The Science and Art of Being Human

This book is

dedicated to all those countless souls

who are

generating,

applying

and diffusing

their knowledge

according to their talents and abilities,

with the sole purpose of shouldering

their individual responsibility

to build a prosperous world civilization.

Because

justice

demands

universal participation.

The Science and Art of Being Human

Questioning accepted understandings
. . . a Bahá'í perspective

Margaret Appa

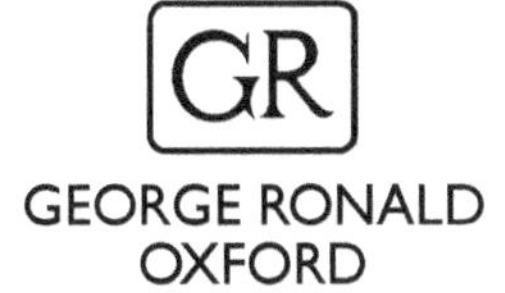

GEORGE RONALD
OXFORD

George Ronald, Publisher
Oxford
www.grbooks.com

A catalogue record for this book is available from the British Library

ISBN 978-0-85398-669-0

Cover design Steiner Graphics

Contents

Acknowledgements

There are many people in my life who have been a part of this project, but perhaps the one I should mention first is my father, John Wade, who was a constant inspiration for me, always questioning, inquiring, wanting to know, wanting to understand. Later in his life when we had both returned to the United Kingdom after many years elsewhere, we had numerous conversations about a myriad of subjects, and I know that it would have been a dream for him to publish a book, and I feel in my heart that he has been an integral part of my efforts to make this happen.

My husband and my children and their families who have all encouraged me, contributed in countless ways to this endeavour and listened patiently to numerous explanations as the ideas have evolved over time.

All Academy participants who over the years were instrumental in my journey of understanding. Through their participation and many enlightening conversations, I grew in my comprehension and ability to articulate the concepts.

All those groups, who during lockdown in 2020/21 invited me to share the ideas with them on Zoom, and from whom I learned and also discovered more unanswered questions to explore.

Those dear friends and family who contributed so willingly to Chapter 6, demonstrating to me that the concepts did make sense to others as well.

There are numerous individuals involved in those years of learning who must be mentioned:

Cecilia Smith, without whose friendship and partnership in adventures together, the Academy would never have happened.

Natasha Wilkinson, who is also family, who was integral to the Academy adventure, and with whom I had many initial conversations and discussions about the themes in the book.

Thelma Batchelor, a lifelong friend, who has always been beside me, encouraging me and has also been the sounding board as I was developing the Zoom presentations that became the structure of the book, and who also read the early manuscript.

Phil Koomen who again has always supported, encouraged and motivated me to keep exploring and finding out and pushing the boundaries.

Beverley Matthews, with whom I have had many conversations, and who has constantly supported and encouraged me.

Barney Leith, who read the first early draft, and encouraged me to continue.

Vafa Ram, who was always there at the Academy, encouraging the team, and later listening patiently to my excitement about the concepts I was uncovering.

Alison Hall, a long-time friend and mentor, who has always been there for me, ready to listen and contribute deeper thinking and initiate further questions that needed answering.

May at George Ronald for offering me the opportunity to publish and the encouragement to complete the manuscript, when I wasn't sure if it was worth doing, and her sterling work in helping me to bring it all together.

And finally, Sir Ken Robinson, through his numerous books and presentations that have inspired, informed, motivated and encouraged me to put into practice ideas that I connected with, and totally understood in terms of how and why they worked so positively in practice.

Introduction

The origins of this journey of exploration are numerous, but the starting point was a question, or rather several questions, and questions require answers or at the very least investigation.

Another origin was my own life experience in arts and education, and how always being considered 'talented' rather than 'intelligent' gave me a mindset about myself which excluded what I understood at the time as 'intelligence', but led to wanting to know why and how this had happened.

My beliefs as a Bahá'í also encouraged me to view the world, as if from space, as a small globe of land and sea where people live, just one people – humankind, and the concept of unity in diversity, the connectedness of all things on the planet. This connectedness on all levels, whether that be the interdependence of all living creatures with the environment, or the earth within the universe, encourages me to bring all aspects of life together, to create unity rather than dichotomies.

Spiritual inspiration

This is my starting point:

> To read the writings of the Faith and to strive to obtain a more adequate understanding of the significance of Bahá'u'lláh's stupendous Revelation are obligations laid on every one of His followers. All are enjoined to delve into the ocean of His Revelation and to partake, in keeping with their capacities and inclinations, of the pearls of wisdom that lie therein.[1]

> . . . there are certain fundamental concepts that all should bear in mind. One is the centrality of knowledge to social existence. The perpetuation of ignorance is a most grievous form of oppression; it reinforces the many walls of prejudice that stand as barriers to the realization of the oneness of humankind, at once the goal and operating principle of Bahá'u'lláh's Revelation. Access to knowledge is the right of every human being, and participation in its generation, application and diffusion a responsibility that all must shoulder in the great enterprise of building a prosperous world civilization, each individual according to his or her talents and abilities. Justice demands universal participation.[2]

The first statement gave me the impetus to explore my beliefs and gain a deeper understanding, particularly in relation to my own passions in life. The second statement encapsulates what I believe about the capacity of every human being: that every individual can be an active participant in generating, applying and diffusing knowledge with the overall goal of building a prosperous world civilization. We all have capacity and abilities, and in the cause of justice we all need to be included.

No one is excluded from this major undertaking. We all contribute according to our unique aptitudes and capacities. No one should be labelled capable /incapable / able /not able; the only limiting factor is the willpower and opportunity of each human being to realise their potential and to know their responsibility.

How does this statement apply to a dialogue on the science and art of being human? This will become clear as we explore the themes.

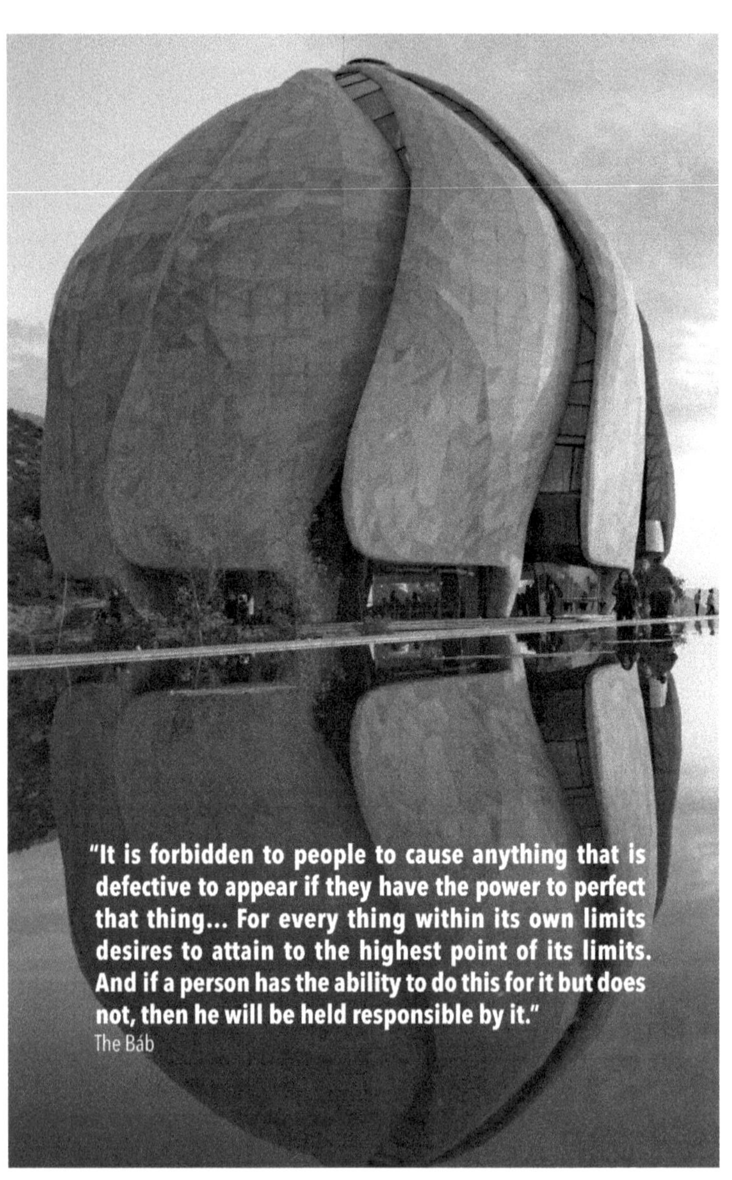
"It is forbidden to people to cause anything that is defective to appear if they have the power to perfect that thing... For every thing within its own limits desires to attain to the highest point of its limits. And if a person has the ability to do this for it but does not, then he will be held responsible by it."
The Báb

1 Art and Artists

What does the word 'art' mean?

There are the liberal arts, defined in the *Encyclopaedia Britannica* as follows:

> . . . the liberal arts include the study of literature, languages, philosophy, history, mathematics, and science as the basis of a general, or liberal, education. Sometimes the liberal-arts curriculum is described as comprehending study of three main branches of knowledge: the humanities (literature, language, philosophy, the fine arts, and history), the physical and biological sciences and mathematics, and the social sciences.

This definition seems to include everything in the curriculum in one hit, but is this how the word 'art' is more usually understood? More commonly, art would be described as:

- *Expression or application of human creative skill typically understood as painting, sculpture, and so on*
- *Works produced by human creative skill or imagination*
- *Various branches of creative activity: the visual, written and performing arts*
- *A skill in a specified thing acquired through practice, e.g. the art of conversation*

What are the historical language roots of the word 'art'?

In exploring the various language traditions of the world, we find that the word 'art', whether in Arabic or the Indo-European, Latin or Greek languages, means a skill or ability. The following is a quotation from a piece of research by Ludwig Tuman exploring art and spirituality; it refers to the language of the original Bahá'í writings and comments on the meaning of arts and science in terms of these languages:

> In the Bahá'í Writings, the words that have been translated as 'art' are usually Arabic *san'at*, Arabic *fan*, and occasionally Persian *hunar*. In the time of Bahá'u'lláh and 'Abdu'l-Bahá, all three of these terms had a very broad sense that included virtually any kind of learned skill or ability. They refer both to arts that involve a kind of activity, such as the art of consultation, and to arts that result in a product. And within the group of products, they refer as much to the arts of brick-laying and cooking as to the arts of poetry and dance.
>
> 'Science,' as referred to in the languages used by Bahá'u'lláh and 'Abdu'l-Bahá, has an equally broad meaning: it implies any search for knowledge, while 'art' implies any skillful application of knowledge. Although these are not complete definitions of science and art, they allow us to understand what was intended in the original language. From this point of view, we can think of any organized body of knowledge as 'a science', and any skill that can be taught as 'an art'.[1]

In the western world the word 'art' comes from two Latin roots:

1. **'Artem',** which means a 'skill' that usually refers to the quality or expressions of what is beautiful, or of great significance. For instance, the word artefact refers to an object of cultural interest made by a human being because: arte: by skill; factum: to make.

2. **'Ars',** which means skill /craft/power, sometimes described as a skill that can be learned.

The word 'artist' is from the same root, and means someone who has a skill. Historically this included a very broad range of skills that would have included professors, those in the industrial trades, and builders, bakers, calligraphers, stonemasons, painters, etc. very much broader than we would consider as being 'artists' today. It truly expressed the meaning as a 'person with a skill'. The skill was not limited. The word 'artisan' is also from Latin roots 'artire' which means to instruct in the arts.

Intriguingly, the word 'skill' also derives from the late Old English 'scele', meaning knowledge, which itself derives from Old Norse 'skil', meaning discernment and knowledge. 'Expert 'derives from the Latin *expertus*, a person who is very knowledgeable about or skilful in a particular area.

So, historically, the words art, skill, knowledge and expertise are interchangeable and very broad in meaning! This will be pertinent as we continue to explore meaning and understanding.

Ask the ordinary person on the street what they understand by the term 'arts' and they will generally respond: 'painting, drawing, drama, singing, dance, writing, plus perhaps the arts in terms of geography, history, philosophy, etc,' as supported by the definition above. The arts are commonly understood as coming under the heading of the visual arts, the performing arts and the written arts. Under these headings are numerous subheadings, but they all relate back to the three main areas of 'art', as generally understood.

Is this understanding upheld by the history of language over time?

Meaning over time in the western languages

The meaning of the word 'art' has changed over time. The following gives a brief overview of the changes.

> Early 1200: 'skill as a result of learning or practice', from Old French *art* (10c.), from Latin *artem* (nominative *ars*): 'work of art; practical skill; a business, craft';
>
> 1300s: in Middle English, usually with a sense of 'skill in scholarship and learning', especially in the seven sciences, or liberal arts. This sense remains in Bachelor of Arts, etc. meaning 'human workmanship' (as opposed to nature);
>
> Late 1500s: 'system of rules and traditions for performing certain actions';
>
> Early 1600s onwards: 'skill in creative arts';
>
> From the 1660s: especially of painting, sculpture, etc.

In the Arabic and Persian languages, it should be noted, art still holds to its original meaning of skill or ability, and therefore includes a very broad range of skills including rug making, house building, painting, calligraphy, tool making, music, dance, agriculture, poetry, teaching, glasswork, and mass produced and industrial items. In other words, anything that requires a skill to produce is a work of art or skill.

Why the change over time in the western traditions? Was there a specific reason for this change? In the 1300s the meaning was broad and inclusive but by the early years of the 1700s it had narrowed to mean what we understand as the fine arts . . . painting, sculpture, drawing, etc.

The explanation for this was the emergence in Europe of the Age of Reason, also known as the Enlightenment. The Age of Reason was an intellectual and cultural movement in the 1700s that dominated ideas, emphasizing reason over superstition and science over blind faith. Beginning in Europe and spreading quickly to America, the concept of the importance of science as a means to understand the world, using methodical and systematic processes, took hold. It became dominant, and the inventions and discoveries that emerged grabbed the imagination of society. It was exciting and new. The arts, on the other hand, were seen as associated with the Church, and were based on emotions, feelings and intuition, superstition and blind faith, at a time when the authority of the Church was also being questioned.

During this period, science, the pursuit of knowledge based on methodical systematic experimentation, became dominant, and the Church authorities, that had up until then claimed the authority of 'knowledge' based on religious doctrine, began to lose respect in the face of these new ideas.

Thus, as the education system was being set up at this time in Europe it absorbed this emphasis and science became dominant alongside the traditions of grammar and the classics. The 'arts' at this stage were not part of the curriculum, and would not be evident until much later.

The Age of Reason, then, was the impetus behind the narrowing of understanding of art to mean the fine arts of sculpture, painting, drawing, and so on.

The artist as understood in the western world

An artist is understood as someone who practises the arts, referring to the commonly understood meaning rather than the liberal arts. The majority of people would quite emphatically state that they are not 'artists' because they cannot draw, paint, dance, sing, write, act or play a musical instrument, and would also believe that this is a 'talent' which is innate, so cannot be learned. The arts and artists are set apart from the ordinary person. Despite an admiration of 'artists' as people with a 'special talent', there is a strange opposite attitude when it comes to the value of the arts and artists in society. In education, for example, the focus is on 'academic' achievement, so the arts, seen as vocational, are not equally valued. This is illustrated when decisions have to be made in times of financial hardship in schools. It is the arts that are cut, not the sciences. Sciences are indispensable while the arts are dispensable!

When considering a career choice, the arts are deemed to

demand less intelligence than the sciences. Those studying the arts at university level are seen to have it easy, their courses are perceived as less demanding, an 'easy option' in relation to the science options. Traditionally art, in terms of learning the skills involved, was not a subject studied at university; those taking this route went to study the visual, dramatic or musical arts at colleges dedicated to these areas, and received diplomas, not degrees! Art at university would be about the theory of art, for example the History of Art, not the practice. This is so strange; art is valued and treasured on one level and denigrated on the other.

The word artist means a person with a skill, so are we saying that only those who practise the visual, performance or written arts have 'skills'? Surely not. We all have skills, a huge variety in a vast array of areas of learning. Skill is also defined as expertise: just look at the number of ways expertise is defined in *Thesaurus.com* as:

> Ability, competence, facility, knowhow, proficiency, prowess, savvy, skilfulness, adroitness, aptness, art, cleverness, craft, deftness, dexterity, expertise, finesse, ingeniousness, mastery.

Surely this includes us all; every single individual can relate to one or more of these definitions in our daily lives or occupations

What are your skills in life?

You might be a teacher, writer, engineer, musician, banker, doctor, singer, chemist, weaver, manager, parent, physicist, dancer, tailor, designer, facilitator, gardener, furniture maker, farmer, mathematician, painter, architect, policeman, nurse . . .

Whatever your occupation, career, lifelong love, you will have multiple related skills. Some of these skills you will use to create objects, in other words the outcome of your skill can be touched or held, they are physical objects such as paintings, houses, gardens, suits, bridges, woven textiles, books, furniture, food, etc.

Some of these skills you will use to create experiences, in other words the outcome of your skill is experienced by others but cannot be touched or held – such as dance, workplaces, classrooms, conversations, homes, music, well-being, facilitation, consultation.

We all have skills and abilities. We all create objects and / or experiences. Then we are all artists or people with skills. This is a radical shift in meaning from the narrow meaning that came about as a result of the Age of Reason.

We use our skills throughout our lives, to create objects and experiences for either the pure joy of creating, or for monetary benefit, or for the benefit of the world we live in.

Do we then, all of us, as artists, people who create the world we inhabit, have a responsibility in how we approach our creative lives and occupations? Is it important that we always strive to do our best in whatever we create, be that a meal for the family or designing a means of reaching the planet Mars?

A Bahá'í perspective on art and artists

I would like to offer a particular perspective on this question, one that emerges from my understanding of the Bahá'í teachings. The Bahá'í writings place skills or arts on a very high level. However, we should remember that in the language of the time these were written, art meant a very broad range of skills that was inclusive of almost everything that was made, fashioned or created.

The following excerpts from the Bahá'í writings were written in the nineteenth century in Persia. They offer a clue to how arts or skills are understood in the Bahá'í Faith. Reading them offers a different perspective from the one with which we are familiar, but one which is inspiring and motivates thinking about art and artists in a totally different way.

> One of the names of God is the Fashioner. He loveth

> craftsmanship. Therefore any of His servants who manifesteth this attribute is acceptable in the sight of this Wronged One. Craftsmanship is a book among the books of divine sciences, and a treasure among the treasures of His heavenly wisdom. This is a knowledge with meaning, for some of the sciences are brought forth by words and come to an end with words.[2]

What might this be saying? Firstly, what is craftsmanship? The *Oxford English Dictionary* defines it as follows:

- Noun [mass noun] skill in a particular craft: e.g. I admire his engineering skills and craftsmanship.

- The quality of design and work shown in something made by hand; artistry: e.g. a piece of fine craftsmanship.

The first example refers to the skills involved, whereas the second refers, in this case, to the object produced as a result of the skills. However, I would consider the term 'craftsmanship' to apply to either an object or an experience.

This definition could be applied to anything that we, as human beings, create . . . think of the design of an aircraft, a vaccine for a pandemic, a prosthetic limb, a children's playground, a plate of food, or a dance performance.

What I am attempting to express here is that I believe that the concept of craftsmanship applies not only to weaving baskets, watchmaking, rug making, furniture and jewellery making . . . it is about everything we as humans create in the world, whether that is actually made by hand or by machines created by the imagination and intelligence of man.

The statement above also refers to craftmanship as 'a book among the books of divine sciences, and a treasure among the treasures of His heavenly wisdom'. This places craftsmanship on the same level as science or knowledge, a divine science no less. (The word 'divine' has its roots in the Latin *divinus* or *divus*, meaning Godlike). This is not how we generally understand craftsmanship. Craftsmanship is not a word we would normally use in referring, for example, to a work of 'science'! This is a challenging statement asking us to think differently about both art and science as we generally understand it.

I had never considered an artist as having a specific responsibility, because my understanding (in the traditional limited sense) was that artists should have absolute freedom to express their inner convictions. They should not be tied by rules, as they are the means by which society is understood over time. They should be 'free spirits', and to some extent, rebels with a cause. However, the following statements by the Báb, the precursor of Baha'u'llah, the founder of the Bahá'í Faith, suggest an alternative understanding.

> No created thing shall ever attain its paradise unless it appeareth in its highest prescribed degree of perfection. For instance, this crystal representeth the paradise of the stone whereof its substance is composed. Likewise, there are various stages in the paradise for the crystal itself . . . So long as it was stone it was worthless, but if it attaineth the excellence of ruby – a potentiality which is latent in it – how much a carat will it be worth? Consider likewise every created thing.[3]

This statement seems to suggest that everything has a need, a yearning to be perfect, using the example of a ruby, which begins as a valueless stone and becomes a rough ruby, then if mined, cut and polished, displays its perfection. It also indicates that every created thing has its own potential, just like the stone that becomes a polished ruby. Might 'every created thing' refer to the whole range of what is created, be that the natural world, or the creations of mankind? Everything has its potential for perfection or its own 'paradise'.

In another place the Báb states:

> Whoever possesseth power over anything must elevate it to its uttermost perfection that it not be deprived of its own

> paradise. For example, the paradise of a sheet of paper on which a few excellent lines are inscribed is that it be refined with patterns of gold illumination, adornment, and excellence that are customary for the most exalted parchment scrolls. Then the possessor of that paper hath elevated it to its utmost degree of glory. Should he know of a higher degree of refinement and fail to manifest it upon that paper, he would deprive it of its paradise, and he would be held accountable, for why hast thou, despite the possession of the means, withheld the effusion of grace and favour?[4]

Is the Báb conveying that it is the responsibility of the 'artist' to bring the medium or material being used to its perfection? The example is of a piece of paper and in this case the art of calligraphy and decoration or illumination.

What is powerful about this statement is that it refers to 'whoever possesseth power', which could refer to anyone, as we all possess power over what we create, be that cooking a meal, writing a story, building a house, singing a song, producing a painting or designing a vehicle. It also suggests that the creator, the person with the skills, is not the important one in this partnership.

Does this change the relationship between the creator and their work? Does this place a responsibility on every one of us to strive always to do our best to enable the medium to come to its perfection?

The end of the statement then goes on to say that if you had the capacity to do something better, and you didn't, then you would be held responsible, you are 'accountable', and the question would be posed as to 'why didn't you?'

Imagine if humanity had this approach, this attitude of mind in creating the world we inhabit. Never doing less than your best, always striving to bring to perfection the materials being used. The Báb in another chapter of the Bayán states:

> It is forbidden to people to cause anything that is defective to appear if they have the power to perfect that thing. For

> example, if someone were to build a house and not bring it to whatever perfection it is capable of achieving, then there will not be an instant that the angels will not be calling out to God for his punishment, even the atoms of that building will also do this. For every thing within its own limits desires to attain to the highest point of its limits. And if a person has the ability to do this for it but does not, then he will be held responsible by it.[5]

Again, this statement clearly defines the responsibility of 'people', which seems to infer anyone, not a particular group of people with particular capacities. The example of the house is an interesting one, conjuring up fascinating images of the atoms of substandard houses crying out for the builders to be punished!

However, this raises the question of how we understand perfection. The Báb clarifies this succinctly in the following text:

> It is not permitted to anyone to write a single letter of the Bayán except in the most beautiful of handwritings. ‹Most beautiful' here means the best that each individual is capable of; not beyond that, but not less than that either . . .
>
> However, all this is on the condition that one keeps within one's capacity, not that one should put oneself in hardship on account of anything. For God desires not to look upon a believer in grief or distress. No! Rather everyone should carry out these obligations according to their ability.[6]

The achievement of perfection is not about exterior standards, it is about each person doing their best, that is all that is demanded: 'not beyond that, but not less than that either'.

The second paragraph emphasizes that we can only do what our unique individual capacity allows us to do, we should not feel hardship or grief or distress, only do our best in everything we do.

Finally, the Báb sets these ideas in a context of our universe:

> Say! We verily have perfected Our handiwork in the creation of the heavens, earth, whatever lieth between them, and in all things; will ye not then behold?. . . Perfect ye then your own handiwork in all that ye produce with your hands working through the handiwork of God. Then would this indeed be a handiwork of God, the Help in Peril, the Self Subsisting. Waste ye not that which God createth with your hands through your handiwork; rather, make manifest in them the perfection of industry or craft, be it a large and mass product or a small and retail one. For verily one who perfecteth his handiwork indeed attaineth certitude in the perfection of the handiwork of God within his own being.[7]

Is this asking us to firstly recognize the perfection of the universe? Then secondly to match this perfection in our own efforts to create our world? The reference to perfection of 'industry or craft', suggests the breadth of meaning, and not wasting what capacity we have through the bounty of God, indicating perhaps that we need to recognize that our capacity is boundless.

This is a fascinating concept; we can apply it to anything that is 'created', be that a building, a drawing, a piece of music, a table, a conversation, a garden, etc. Imagine if this were understood and put into practice by those using their 'art', where the 'art' is the skill used to apply their knowledge – what an aesthetically beautiful and refined world we would live within.

To a Bahá'í the perfect example of this is the gardens that have been created on Mount Carmel in the Holy Land, the administrative and spiritual centre of the world Bahá'í community. The mountain has been brought to its perfection by a team of people who, over many years, applied to the highest standards of which they were capable their combined knowledge and multiple skills.

A beautifully crafted piece of furniture, an elegantly timeless building, an exquisite painting, an inspiring piece of research, a carefully presented plate of food, a mathematical equation that resolves an age-old question . . . these all demand a 'bringing to perfection' of the elements being used, and an application of knowledge that draws the response of delight and awe or pleasure from the viewer or consumer.

In summary

If we recognize that every human being has skills and capacities, then the meaning of art and artists becomes broad and inclusive, rather than narrow and exclusive.

If we accept that the Báb, in referring to those with a responsibility to use their capacities to the very best of their ability, is referring to everyone, not just a chosen few, then we have to recognize that we all have a responsibility to make sure that whatever medium we are using – words, wood, sounds, numbers, food, metal, paint, ideas, paper, plants, animals, movement, textiles, people, glass, clay – is brought to its perfection, its particular paradise, as the Báb says, 'for why hast thou, despite the possession of the means, withheld the effusion of grace and favour?' And, as quoted in the Introduction, the Universal House of Justice writes:

> Access to knowledge is the right of every human being, and participation in its generation, application and diffusion a responsibility that all must shoulder in the great enterprise of building a prosperous world civilization, each individual according to his or her talents and abilities. Justice demands universal participation.[8]

The Universal House of Justice states clearly that every human being is involved in the 'generation, application and diffusion' of knowledge, indeed: 'Justice demands universal participation.'

So how do we understand 'knowledge'? How does this question relate to the arts discussed in this chapter?

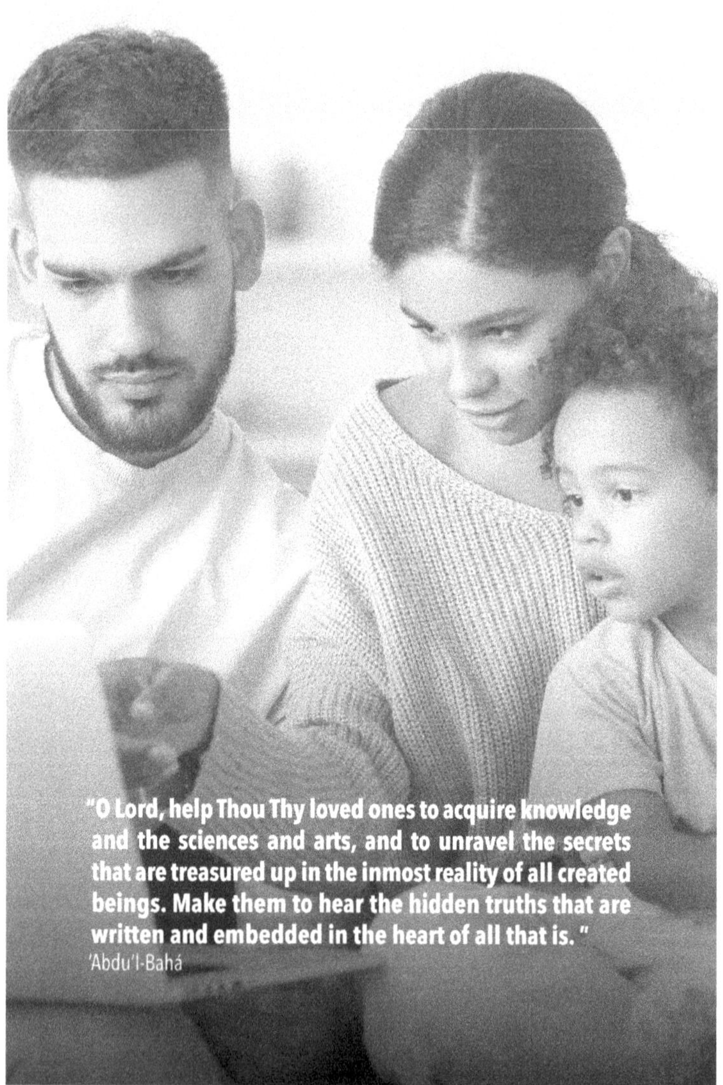
"O Lord, help Thou Thy loved ones to acquire knowledge and the sciences and arts, and to unravel the secrets that are treasured up in the inmost reality of all created beings. Make them to hear the hidden truths that are written and embedded in the heart of all that is."
'Abdu'l-Bahá

2 Science and Art

An alternative definition of art and artists has been suggested that does not exclude what is now considered art, but expands it to include the creative capacity of every human being who designs, makes, fashions, creates all those objects and experiences that mankind has devised, that is our world – our homes, our cities, our means of travel on the planet and beyond, to the creative capacity of parents applying their hard-won skills to raising the next generation, to those who labour tirelessly to keep the nation fed, healthy, educated and safe.

The list of skills is endless, and from this alternative perspective a person with skills and capacity is an artist; every single person is applying their skills in their life circumstances.

So where does science fit into this dialogue? How then is science understood?

The ordinary person in the street would say that science is about physics, chemistry, biology, engineering, and so on, but our dictionaries define science as:

- intellectual and practical activity encompassing the systematic study of the structure and behaviour of the physical and natural world through observation and experiment; or

- a systematically organized body of knowledge on a particular subject.

If the historical roots of the word 'science' are explored, then the following emerges:

Archaic:	knowledge of any kind
Middle English:	from old French denoting knowledge,
Latin:	scientia, from scire 'to know'; knowledge, a knowing, an expertness
Indo-European	gno, to know
Greek:	gnoscere, from gnosis – knowledge
Arabic:	'ilm, the Islamic term for knowledge.

The word 'science' has its roots, no matter which language is selected, in the word 'knowledge'.

Scientist

The word 'scientist' was invented in 1834 by Cambridge University historian and philosopher of science William Whewell to replace such terms as 'cultivators of science'. He wanted to match words like artist, atheist, humanist. But the word 'scientist' that is now used as a demonstration of 'truth and proof' is problematic, especially when historically the term 'artist' also encompasses knowledge and skills and expertise. So, has the random invention of the word scientist come to mean something more than it actually should?

Science, as an area of learning, is seen as demanding of intelligence rather than talent, yet as with artists, scientists are placed on a pedestal, seen as a group apart. 'Ordinary' people often would not see themselves as having the 'intelligence' to be a scientist. Thus, within our society art and science are seen as oppositional, particularly within the education system where young people are channelled into either 'the arts' or 'the sciences'. For some reason this relationship is not questioned; it is an accepted truth that science and art are unrelated and separate areas of learning. But are they?

Meaning of the word 'knowledge' over time

Over time language meanings change, and science is no exception. Here is a very brief summary:

> From c.1400: 'experiential knowledge'; also, a skill, handicraft; a trade.
>
> 1670s: in the sense of 'non-arts studies'.
>
> 1725: the modern (restricted) sense of 'body of regular or methodical observations or propositions concerning a particular subject or speculation'.

Language understanding over time demonstrates that in the 1400s the words art and science had a similar meaning. Both were understood as involving knowledge and skills, there was no dichotomy! Now in the 21st century we have quite fixed ideas about their separateness.

Science is perceived as being:
- For the academic learner
- For the intelligent
- A safe choice of career
- A guarantee of an income
- Indispensable

Art is perceived as being:
- For the vocational learner
- For the talented
- A risky choice of career
- No guarantee of an income
- Dispensable

In a presentation to the Association of Bahá'í Studies conference in the United States in September 2017, Mr Hooper Dunbar, a former member of the Universal House of Justice, and a recognized and respected painter in oils, gave a presentation on the occasion of the bicentenary of Bahá'u'lláh. About 25 minutes into the talk, he stopped and made the following statement:

> I am going to interrupt for a second to say something I wanted to share with regard to art.
>
> In Haifa we put together a compilation on science and art, and as you examine the original writings you find that science is knowledge and art is application or technology.
>
> 'Abdu'l-Bahá calls industry art, 'Abdu'l-Bahá calls agriculture art. If you think of this wonderful phrase –the artist is the source of everything – in a little broader context, it doesn't eliminate the fine arts, the fine arts are right there. He talks about the painter with the brush, it does extend, so if you don't happen to be good at painting or sculpture or modern dance, don't despair, go on with your service to mankind through application of science, through the application of knowledge.
>
> There's a list of what 'Abdu'l-Bahá calls arts, it includes just about everything that you could do in the world.[1]

Mr Dunbar states that the compilation on science and art he refers to indicates that '*Science is knowledge and art is the application of knowledge or the application of science.*'

This is a challenging statement that turns upside down our present understanding. Taken literally, it seems not to make sense. How can painting, sculpture, drawing, music or drama be the application of chemistry, physics and biology? There must be an alternative way of interpreting this relationship, and I propose a different approach.

As we have seen, science in terms of the historical roots in language means knowledge. Art in terms of the historical roots in language means a skill or ability. Note also that in the language of the Báb, Baha'u'lláh and 'Abdu'l-Bahá, these were the meanings, and remain so today.

Imagine if . . .

Imagine if, for one moment, we were to put aside the accepted interpretation and use the words 'knowledge' and 'skill', rather than 'science' and 'art'. Where might this lead us?

Consider the following: nursing, design, teaching, gardening, parenting, engineering, architecture, poetry, acting, chemistry, retail, music . . . Any of these can be an occupation, a career, or a lifetime love. Can it be imagined in any of these examples that there be only theory . . . the knowledge of the subject? Would the theory, on its own, produce an outcome? Isn't it the skills that allow the theory to be applied in practice?

Think about your own knowledge and your own skills. Ask yourself how they connect together. Is it enough to have just knowledge? Could the skills be how you apply your knowledge? 'Abdu'l-Bahá said:

> All the heavenly Books, divine Prophets, sages and philosophers agree that warfare is destructive to human development, and peace constructive. They agree that war and strife strike at the foundations of humanity. Therefore, a power is needed to prevent war and to proclaim and establish the oneness of humanity.
>
> But knowledge of the need of this power is not sufficient. Realizing that wealth is desirable is not becoming wealthy. The admission that scientific attainment is praiseworthy does not confer scientific knowledge. Acknowledgement of the excellence of honour does not make a man honourable. Knowledge of human conditions and the needed remedy for them is not the cause of their betterment. To admit that health is good does not constitute health. A skilled physician is needed to remedy existing human conditions. As a physician is required to have complete knowledge of pathology, diagnosis, therapeutics and treatment, so this World Physician must be wise, skilful and capable before health will result. His mere knowledge is not health; it must be applied and the remedy carried out.

> The attainment of any object is conditioned upon knowledge, volition and action. Unless these three conditions are forthcoming, there is no execution or accomplishment.[2]

Knowledge on its own, then, achieves nothing. There must be the will or volition to make something happen, and then that knowledge has to be applied through action, which logically demands skills. Would it then be logical to say that skills are the means for knowledge to be applied? Would it then be logical to say that art is the application of science?

Viewed from this alternative perspective, we could say that our daily lives are an expression of an intrinsic connection between science and art. Here are a few examples:

- Doctors study the science of medicine, but the application of that science in whatever field of practice is an art.
- The science of architecture when applied to creating a building results in a work of art.
- Parents have no training, they learn their science on the job, but it results in the art of parenting.
- The science of horticulture results in beautiful gardens and parks – surely works of art.
- The art of music is founded on the science or theory underpinning it.
- The sculptor's works of art are founded on the result of many years of building an understanding of the science.
- The science of research demands the art of communication in order that complex data can be understood by others.

This model of thinking can be applied to any occupation or profession, or to simply living life, and it seems to make sense. Science (knowledge) is a universal resource which we acquire, but without the perfection of art (skills) to apply it in practice, it serves no real purpose.

Does this not indicate that every individual has a unique combination of science and art, or knowledge and skills, and that there is no dichotomy? I would suggest that it is not the label 'scientist' or 'artist' that gives us permission to use these capacities; as human beings we all acquire knowledge and can perfect the expertise or skill to apply that knowledge. The problem is not with the words but with how we understand them.

Thought of in this way, art *is* the application of science, but only if the understanding of both science and art is broad and inclusive, where science is seen as any system of knowledge and art any form of application that enables that system of knowledge to be applied in practice.

The interconnectedness of knowledge

Chris Anderson, the CEO of TED, explains in his book *TED Talks: The Official TED Guide to Public Speaking* (2018) how he attended a TED conference that had been recommended by a friend, and how by day three his brain 'began sparking like a lightning storm' because of the stimulation of ideas coming from the quick-fire presentations on a broad range of topics, and how ideas from very different presentations began to connect together. One presentation affected him deeply; he realized that 'it was possible to own your own future. No matter what life had served you, you could find a way to shape it, and in so doing make a difference for others too.' He had realized that by sharing knowledge and experiences, intricate connections are created from which we all can learn and benefit. All knowledge is interconnected.[3]

He refers to a book he was reading at the time, *The Fabric of Reality* by David Deutsch. This book posed a question about knowledge, describing how we live in a world where it seems we are expected to become more and more specialized in particular areas of knowledge. The author poses a question about the relationship between knowledge and understanding, and suggests that understanding comes by 'moving in the opposite direction', becoming less specialized, and pursuing the 'unification of knowledge'. Anderson explores this in the context of TED and concludes that all knowledge is connected into a gigantic web. When this web is viewed close up to reveal one small connection or area of knowledge, the beauty of the connectivity of the whole is lost. It was this access to the connectedness of all knowledge that was inspiring and sparked more and more ideas.

Anderson goes on to describe our education system as a leftover from the industrial age, and says that we are now moving into a knowledge economy where 'specialist knowledge traditionally wielded by humans is being taken over by computers'. The whereabouts of oil deposits and the diagnosis of some complex medical conditions can now be answered far more quickly and efficiently by computers than by man.

As this world becomes a reality, it offers the opportunity to use our unique capacities of humanness to create an exciting world where, as Chris Anderson suggests, we will have more creativity, more innovation and more 'utilization of uniquely human values.' In this world we will require a different sort of knowledge: it won't be about what we know, but how knowledge is used within specific contexts. We will need creative knowledge and a deeper understanding of our own humanity.

Anderson writes: 'the knowledge era we are entering demands a different type of knowledge, encouraging people to be inspired by those outside their traditional specialities, and in so doing to develop a deeper understanding of their world and their role in it.' This thinking process led Anderson to understand that TED was 'not really just the synergy between technology, entertainment, and design. It was actually the connectedness of **all** knowledge'.[4]

What does knowledge look like?

Anderson describes knowledge visually as a web, possibly a web that is a globe where every single strand is connected to every other strand. Another conception of knowledge is to visualize it as a rope. Richard J. Bernstein, in his book *Beyond Objectivism and Relativism*, discusses the meaning of knowledge, stating that 'Knowledge is not conceived as an exact description of reality, but involves insights into reality that can guide effective practice'. He goes on to explain: 'It is not a bedrock, but as a rope in which insights are like the fibres,' and describes that rather than science as the prototype of all knowledge, knowledge is more like a rope made up of strands of everyone's experiences, the source of each strand is unknown, but it contributes to one strong cord, which as lives evolve and adapt and change, so does the learning evolve over time. He suggests that we are all contributing to this rope of knowledge.

This concept of knowledge as a rope that flows through society and over time reflects the understanding of an evolving world, is interesting in the context of this discussion. An interconnected global web or an ever-growing rope are images that might help us to visualize and understand what knowledge is. However, knowledge on its own is not enough, as argued previously. It is the application of knowledge, using the relevant skills, that produces outcomes that are visible and useful to humanity.

The Bahá'í perspective

Do the Bahá'í writings offer any clues as to how we might understand the relationship between science and art and the meaning of knowledge? Bahá'u'lláh writes:

> Arts, crafts and sciences uplift the world of being, and are conducive to its exaltation. Knowledge is as wings to man's life, and a ladder for his ascent. Its acquisition is incumbent upon everyone. The knowledge of such sciences, however,

> should be acquired as can profit the peoples of the earth, and not those that begin with words and end with words. Great indeed is the claim of scientists and craftsmen on the peoples of the world.
>
> . . . In truth, knowledge is a veritable treasure for man, and a source of glory, of bounty, of joy, of exaltation, of cheer and gladness unto him. Happy the man that cleaveth unto it, and woe betide the heedless.[5]

The use of the analogies of knowledge as wings and ladders for man is intriguing: it seems to suggest that knowledge of itself uplifts and inspires, fascinates, takes us up and beyond what we think we are capable of achieving. But note how the first phrase connects 'arts, crafts and sciences': the connection is obvious within the sphere of this exploration.

'Knowledge is a veritable treasure . . . a source of glory . . .' – there is no indication here of knowledge of any particular kind. This is knowledge broad and inclusive. Also note that since the word 'scientist' was invented only in the mid-1800s, its present meaning would not have been familiar to Bahá'u'lláh when He revealed these words. Elsewhere, He states:

> Knowledge is one of the wondrous gifts of God. It is incumbent upon everyone to acquire it. Such arts and material means as are now manifest have been achieved by virtue of His knowledge and wisdom which have been revealed in Epistles and Tablets through His Most Exalted Pen – a Pen out of whose treasury pearls of wisdom and utterance and the arts and crafts of the world are brought to light.[6]

What is this explaining? It is firstly making a clear connection between knowledge and its application – art. This connection is then reiterated in the final sentence, 'pearls of wisdom and utterance and the arts and crafts of the world are brought to light'.

Bahá'u'lláh states:

> Unveiled and unconcealed, this Wronged One hath, at all

> times, proclaimed before the face of all the peoples of the world that which will serve as the key for unlocking the doors of sciences, of arts, of knowledge, of well-being, of prosperity and wealth.[7]

Note how 'sciences, arts, knowledge, well-being, prosperity and wealth' are all mentioned together. What is the connection? Might it be understood that without science and arts (or knowledge and skills), we would not have well-being, prosperity and wealth?

'Abdu'l-Bahá wrote to a student of agriculture:

> Strive as much as possible to become proficient in the science of agriculture, for in accordance with the divine teachings the acquisition of sciences and the perfection of arts are considered acts of worship. If a man engageth with all his power in the acquisition of a science or in the perfection of an art, it is as if he has been worshipping God in churches and temples. Thus as thou enterest a school of agriculture and strivest in the acquisition of that science thou art day and night engaged in acts of worship – acts that are accepted at the threshold of the Almighty. What bounty greater than this, that science should be considered as an act of worship and art as service to the Kingdom of God.[8]

Note the use of the words 'acquisition of science' and 'perfection of arts'. Might this be indicating how knowledge must be acquired, sought out, found, discovered, while the arts or skills are already present as the 'gems in the inmost mines' that need to be mined and polished and perfected through education? The connection between art and science is again confirmed by the final sentence where science is considered an act of worship and art as service to God. Elsewhere, 'Abdu'l-Bahá writes:

> O ye recipients of the favours of God! In this new and wondrous Age, the unshakable foundation is the teaching of

> sciences and arts. According to explicit Holy Texts, every child must be taught crafts and arts . . . It followeth that whatever soul shall offer his aid to bring this about will assuredly be accepted at the Heavenly Threshold, and extolled by the Company on High.[9]

This is a fascinating statement. Does it really mean that the teaching of the sciences and arts, as we understand it now, is the 'unshakable foundation' of this new and wondrous world? Does it mean that chemistry, physics, biology, etc., and painting, music, writing, sculpture, etc. are the 'unshakable foundations'? I would question that. However, if we understand science and art in the broader context discussed above, then yes, of course, where would the world be without knowledge and skills? 'Abdu'l-Bahá writes:

> See how, in this day the scope of sciences and arts hath widened out, and what wondrous technical advances have been made, and to what a high degree the mind's powers have increased, and what stupendous inventions have appeared.[10]

Again, see how 'Abdu'l-Bahá uses sciences and arts together and links this to inventions, technical advances and the increase in 'the mind's powers' of this time.

> The perpetuation of ignorance is a most grievous form of oppression; it reinforces the many walls of prejudice that stand as barriers to the realization of the oneness of humankind, at once the goal and operating principle of Bahá'u'lláh's Revelation. Access to knowledge is the right of every human being, and participation in its generation, application and diffusion a responsibility that all must shoulder in the great enterprise of building a prosperous world civilization, each individual according to his or her talents and abilities. Justice demands universal participation.[11]

For me this statement by the Universal House of Justice in 2010 confirms the relationship between knowledge and action.

In summary

In this chapter a broad inclusive understanding of the word 'art' has been connected to a broad inclusive understanding of the word 'science'. This relationship then suggests that every individual, according to his or her unique capacities, is responsible to generate, apply and diffuse knowledge in order to build a prosperous world civilization. But what is meant by unique capacities?

"The human soul is to be compared to a weaver; the human life is the thing woven, the cloth; the human body, principally the brain, is the tool, the instrument with which the weaving is done. God the Lord, the Master of the works, prepares the loom, that is the warp for the loom, the human milieu or environment with the ground-threads of fate. Thereby will be forced on the human being, the place, the time, the parents, the religion, nationality, society qualities, that is of gifted persons etc. The human soul then throws across the warp-threads the filling or woof by means of the shuttle that is the five senses, imagination, action, whereby up to the end of life as we say, are developed the masterpieces of the human life...."

'Abdu'l-Bahá

3 Science and Art of Human and Spiritual Capacities

Human capacity

What does it mean to be human? Can we define our unique human capacities? In earlier chapters we have explored knowledge and skills, which are part of our unique capacities; however, creativity and intelligence cannot be separated from the ability to acquire knowledge and to perfect skills.

Intelligences

Historically, intelligence had a single meaning. A person was on a spectrum between being highly intelligent and not intelligent. Intelligence came to be synonymous with academic achievement, and to this day is still widely considered in this way. Academic achievement was connected to academic 'subjects', so to be thought of as intelligent meant success in the academic subjects, whereas success in non-academic subjects was seen as not so much of an achievement. It demanded talent, not intelligence; it was vocational, not academic!

The word 'vocational' has become synonymous with 'training in specific skills for particular occupations', for example fashion, catering, bricklaying, hairdressing. The implicit understanding is that these skills in relation to skills acquired on a course preparing someone for a career in physics, medicine, chemistry, mathematics or engineering are seen as less valuable, demanding less intelligence. Is it the case that in reality, the demands of the skills in either case are simply different, demanding of a different set of intelligences and passions? Just a totally different set of gems to be refined and utilized in service to mankind?

In terms of what they potentially offer to mankind, should they simply be considered as equal in worth?

Sir Ken Robinson suggests that 'academic ability' and 'intelligence' are conflated, and this has been institutionalized across all areas of education. Robinson was the chair of a committee set up by the UK Government 'to make recommendations to the Secretaries of State on the creative and cultural development of young people through formal and informal education: to take stock of current provision and to make proposals for principles, policies and practice'. He writes:

> Many highly intelligent people have passed through the whole of their education feeling that they are not, and many academically able people who've been fêted by the system have never discovered their other abilities.[1]

He suggests that institutions and intellectual hierarchies have been developed on the assumption that there are only two types of people, 'academic and non-academic, or as they are often called . . . the able and the less able'.

However, research has now shown that intelligence is multifaceted. Every human being has a 'basket' of intelligences, which we each have in a unique combination, and they come to define who we are and the potential for what we can do with our lives.

It was Howard Gardner who defined the concept of multiple intelligences, and identified eight, but he did not rule out others that might be identified in the future.[2] They are listed here:

- Linguistic intelligence is a sensitivity to spoken and written language, the ability to learn languages, and the capacity to use language to accomplish certain goals. Writers, poets, lawyers and speakers are among those that have high linguistic intelligence.

- Logical-mathematical intelligence consists of the capacity to analyse problems logically, carry out mathematical operations, and investigate issues methodically. This intelligence is most often associated with scientific and mathematical thinking.

- Musical intelligence involves skill in the performance, composition and appreciation of musical patterns. According to Gardner, musical intelligence runs in an almost structural parallel to linguistic intelligence.

- Bodily-kinaesthetic intelligence entails the potential of using one's whole body or parts of the body to solve problems. It is the ability to use mental abilities to coordinate bodily movements. Dancers, sportsmen and women, and gymnasts in particular have this ability.

- Visual-spatial intelligence involves the potential to recognize and visualize objects and patterns of space, and the ability to think in shapes, images, patterns, designs, and textures, both through our eyes and the imagination. Architects, designers, choreographers and builders all need this intelligence.

- Interpersonal intelligence is concerned with the capacity to understand the intentions, motivations and desires of other people. Educators, salespeople, religious and political leaders, counsellors and medical practitioners all need a well-developed interpersonal intelligence.

- Naturalist intelligence involves the full range of knowing that occurs in and through our encounters with the natural world including our recognition, appreciation and understanding of the natural environment and the wider context of the universe.

- Intra-personal intelligence is fundamentally inward since

> it implies the ability to understand oneself. These people are not only aware of their wishes, feelings, moods and expectations, but they use that information to intelligently manage their lives. Those who possess this type of intelligence understand how their cognitive processes (thinking, attention and memory) work, which allows them to make better decisions and solve problems more effectively.

It appears then that, according to Robinson and Gardner, human capacity is complex and cannot be explained by simple and now outdated terms such as academic /non-academic, intelligent /unintelligent. However, the education 'systems', designed for the convenience of control and management, have not yet recognized the vast potential of every individual to contribute, in multiple ways, to the well-being of the world and its peoples. Robinson suggests that we need to rethink:

> I believe our only hope for the future is to adopt a new conception of human ecology, one in which we start to reconstitute our conception of the richness of human capacity. Our education system has mined our minds in the way that we strip-mine the earth for a particular commodity and for the future, it won't serve us. We have to rethink the fundamental principles on which we are educating our children.[3]

What is creativity?

Ken Robinson has been an inspiration for me, and his record of working within the system to make changes happen, in relation to the arts in education, are well documented. I first read his report *All Our Futures: Creativity, Culture and Education* very soon after it was published in 1999. In this report is the following statement:

> One of our aims in this report is to emphasise the importance of the arts and their essential place in creative

> development. But creativity is not unique to the arts. It is equally fundamental to advances in the sciences, in mathematics, technology, in politics, business and in all areas of everyday life.[4]

The report also states:

> In our view, all people are capable of creative achievement in some area of activity, provided the conditions are right and they have acquired the relevant knowledge and skills.[5]
>
> Creative processes in all disciplines normally involve an initial phase of drafting: of giving an idea a rough shape or outline. This may be the first notes of a melody; a first image or metaphor; the first sketch of a problem in mathematics. The process of development is commonly one of 'successive approximations' in which the idea is shaped and clarified in the process of exploring it. The final phases are often to do with refining the detail of the expression: with producing the neat copy, so to speak. The classical division of stages in creative thought – preparation-incubation-illumination then verification – is contested in various ways by different scholars but it does alert us to the common pattern of focus, withdrawal and then breakthrough and to the key point that creativity is a process, not an event. The form of this withdrawal from thinking about a problem, and the best circumstances for its success, are personal to the individual but often involves waking/sleeping moments, or a 'moving meditation' as we do other things. Creative activity involves a complex combination of controlled and non-controlled elements, unconscious as well as conscious mental processes, non-directed as well as directed thought, intuitive as well as rational calculation.[6]

In February 2015, Warwick University, incidentally the University where Ken Robinson worked at the time of the 1999 report, held a commission of enquiry that resulted in a report titled *Enriching Britain: Culture, Creativity and Growth.* In the section 'An entitlement to a fused STEAM + curriculum', this report suggested that:

> There are major concerns that the educational system is not focussing on the future needs of the Cultural and Creative Industries and the broader needs for innovation and growth in the UK. There is a general agreement within the Cultural and Creative Industries and industry more broadly that the Government's focus on Science, Technology, Engineering and Maths (STEM) should include the Arts (STEAM). However, the Commission shares the concerns of others, including Nesta, that policymakers are obsessed with a siloed subject-based curriculum and early specialisation in Arts or Science disciplines that ignores and obscures discussion around the future need for all children to enjoy an education that encourages creativity, making and enterprise across the curriculum. We need creative scientists as much as we need artists who understand the property of materials and the affordances of new technology.[7]

And elsewhere, Ken Robinson says:

> Creative achievement is related to control of the medium. Simply asking people to be creative is not enough. Children and adults need the means and the skills to be creative. I can't play the piano. I don't mean I'm incapable of playing; I have never learnt how to do it. To that extent I cannot be creative on the piano. I can make noises on it and give vent to my immediate feelings but not be musically creative in the same way as those who can play it.[8]

This concept applies to anything we feel we cannot do, drawing, running, writing, mathematics, chemistry – we do not magically acquire these skills as we get older, just as we do not automatically know how to drive on our seventeenth birthday.

Robinson would say that if you find the thing you love

doing and you are also very good at doing it, then you will be in your element. In a talk given to the RSA *(Royal Society of Arts, Manufacture and Commerce),* Robinson tells the story of a talented musician who had spent her childhood and much of her adulthood becoming a concert pianist, with all the dedication and hard work that entails. After one such concert she was congratulated on her playing by the conductor, but he asked if she enjoyed playing. She replied no, she never 'enjoyed' playing, she could just do it, she was good at it, and it was what she had always done. At the end of that season, with all her commitments fulfilled, she closed the piano lid and never played again – she realized that what she was passionate about was books and writing and reading and being with the people involved in that. She became a literary editor, which was how Robinson had met her. She was then in what Robinson calls 'her element'. In her new life she was creatively engaged in using her skills, intelligence and knowledge, and was enjoying the process.

Robinson suggests that creativity is about 'imaginative processes with outcomes that are original and of value'. He says there is a difference between imagination and creativity, and that is, an outcome: 'You could be imaginative all day long without anyone noticing . . . to be creative you actually have to do something.'

He continues by proposing that creativity applies to 'anything that involves using your intelligence'. We all have multiple intelligences, we all have creative capacity, and creativity is a function of intelligence. This is somewhat different from the accepted understanding that it is only 'artistic individuals' who are creative! In Robinson's words:

> Because being creative involves doing something, it will always involve using some form of media. These may be physical media, such as steel, wood, clay, fabric or food; they may be sensory media, like sound, light, the voice or the body; they may be cognitive media, including words, numbers or notation. Whatever the media, there is an intimate relationship between the ideas and the media through

> which they take shape. This is true whether the task is designing a building, developing a mathematical theorem, a scientific hypothesis or a musical composition. Creativity is a dialogue between the ideas and the media in which they are being formed.[9]

In whatever order the generating or evaluating of ideas happens, there is always an outcome. The medium can be anything at all, it may be a guitar, and/or voices, but it could also be numbers, or a thinking process in the classroom to completely change the day's programme, or it could be playing with ingredients that result in a new pasta sauce for the family's meal, or it could be unexpected ideas triggered by an experience or a poem!

This creative process then involves both the thinking capacities of the brain and the physical potential of the body, it is a dynamic process that might sometimes demand that we relinquish control and actually allow the unconscious 'ruminations of the mind' to produce an answer. Have we not all experienced those moments when we wake up at 3 a.m. and know exactly how to solve that issue we have been struggling with for two days!

What is the role of creativity within this 'science/art' dialogue?

Robinson explores this theme:

> Creativity is not a separate faculty that some people have and others don't, it is not confined to certain sorts of creative activities, like the arts. Creativity is possible in all areas of human activity and it draws from all areas of human intelligence. It is not a strictly logical process in the conventional sense. It draws from intuitions and feelings, as well as from practical knowledge and skill. One of the legacies of the Enlightenment is a division between knowing and feeling, intellect and emotion. This division is illustrated in the common-sense assumptions that are now held about the

> differences between the arts and sciences. The sciences are thought to be about knowledge, facts and objectivity: the arts about emotions, self-expression and being creative. In reality there are many similarities in the creative processes of the arts and sciences. Both have subjective and objective elements and both draw on knowledge, feelings, intuition and non-logical elements.[10]

Can the creative process of thinking and doing be separated from the search for knowledge and the application of that knowledge through expertise or skills? The humble fisherman with his small boat requires knowledge of the sea and the habits of the fish, but to apply his knowledge to best effect, he will be refining and creatively developing the processes he uses to enable him to catch food for his family. The team of experts working together to solve the challenges of climate change will undoubtedly be pooling their unique combination of knowledge and skills. Creative thinking will be essential to this process in both scenarios.

Robinson asked a professional designer who was also a Nobel Prize winner for chemistry what the difference is between creativity in the arts and sciences. Sir Harry Kroto responded:

> The process is the same, even though the outcomes are different. In all creative processes we are pushing the boundaries of what we know now, to explore new possibilities; we are drawing on the skills we have now, often stretching and evolving them as the work demands.[11]

The capacity of the soul

Do we understand what this soul is, how it functions, its capacity, where it resides? What is the connection between the soul and our physical abilities to think, create and fashion the world we inhabit?

'Abdu'l-Bahá offers numerous explanations, a few of which are offered here. At this stage I will offer no comment, but will attempt to make the connection between the capacities of our soul and our human capacities a little later.

> The soul is not a combination of elements, it is not composed of many atoms, it is of one indivisible substance and therefore eternal. It is entirely out of the order of the physical creation; it is immortal![12]
>
> The foremost degree of comprehension in the world of nature is that of the rational soul. This power and comprehension is shared in common by all men, whether they be heedless or aware, wayward or faithful. In the creation of God, the rational soul of man encompasses and is distinguished above all other created things: It is by virtue of its nobility and distinction that it encompasses them all. Through the power of the rational soul, man can discover the realities of things, comprehend their properties, and penetrate the mysteries of existence. All the sciences, branches of learning, arts, inventions, institutions, undertakings, and discoveries have resulted from the comprehension of the rational soul. These were once impenetrable secrets, hidden mysteries, and unknown realities, and the rational soul gradually discovered them and brought them out of the invisible plane into the realm of the visible. This is the greatest power of comprehension in the world of nature, and the uttermost limit of its flight is to comprehend the realities, signs, and properties of contingent things.[13]

> Spirit cannot be perceived by the material senses of the physical body, excepting as it is expressed in outward signs and works. The human body is visible, the soul is invisible. It is the soul nevertheless that directs a man's faculties, that governs his humanity.
>
> The soul has two main faculties. (a) As outer circumstances are communicated to the soul by the eyes, ears, and brain of a man, so does the soul communicate its desires and purposes through the brain to the hands and tongue of the physical body, thereby expressing itself. The spirit in the

soul is the very essence of life. (b) The second faculty of the soul expresses itself in the world of vision, where the soul inhabited by the spirit has its being, and functions without the help of the material bodily senses. There, in the realm of vision, the soul sees without the help of the physical eye, hears without the aid of the physical ear, and travels without dependence upon physical motion. It is, therefore, clear that the spirit in the soul of man can function through the physical body by using the organs of the ordinary senses, and that it is able also to live and act without their aid in the world of vision. This proves without a doubt the superiority of the soul of man over his body, the superiority of spirit over matter.

For example, look at this lamp: is not the light within it superior to the lamp which holds it? However beautiful the form of the lamp may be, if the light is not there its purpose is unfulfilled, it is without life – a dead thing. The lamp needs the light, but the light does not need the lamp.

The spirit does not need a body, but the body needs spirit, or it cannot live. The soul can live without a body, but the body without a soul dies.[14]

When the light of faith is kindled in the lamp of the heart and soul, its spreading rays illumine every limb of the body. When this resplendent light shineth forth through the medium of the tongue, it is made manifest in the powers of speech and utterance. When its beams fall upon the eyes, insight and true vision are revealed, and when it stirreth the ear, it bestoweth attentive hearing. When this light sheddeth its radiance upon the mind, it leadeth to the recognition of the All-Merciful, and when it setteth aglow the limbs, it findeth expression in purity and the worship of God. Otherwise, all physical powers, all limbs and members would remain useless and futile and their actions would fade like a mirage in the desert.[15]

In *Some Answered Questions*, ‘Abdu’l-Bahá addresses the question, 'What is the difference between mind, spirit, and soul?' This passage also describes the relationship between the vegetable, animal and human spirit and the importance of the connection between the human spirit and the spirit of Faith.

> It was already explained that, in general, spirit is divided into five categories: the vegetable spirit, the animal spirit, the human spirit, the spirit of faith, and the Holy Spirit.
>
> The vegetable spirit is that power of growth which is brought about in the seed through the influence of other created things.
>
> The animal spirit is that all-embracing sensory power which is realized through the composition and combination of the elements. When this composition disintegrates, that spirit likewise perishes and becomes non-existent. It may be likened to this lamp: When oil, wick, and flame are brought together and combined, it is lit; and when this combination disintegrates – that is, when the constituent parts are separated from one another – the lamp also is extinguished.
>
> The human spirit, which distinguishes man from the animal, is the rational soul, and these two terms – the human spirit and the rational soul – designate one and the same thing. This spirit, which in the terminology of the philosophers is called the rational soul, encompasses all things and as far as human capacity permits, discovers their realities and becomes aware of the properties and effects, the characteristics and conditions of earthly things. But the human spirit, unless it be assisted by the spirit of faith, cannot become acquainted with the divine mysteries and the heavenly realities. It is like a mirror which, although clear, bright, and polished, is still in need of light. Not until a sunbeam falls upon it can it discover the divine mysteries.
>
> As for the mind, it is the power of the human spirit. The spirit is as the lamp, and the mind as the light that shines from it. The spirit is as the tree, and the mind as the fruit. The mind is the perfection of the spirit and a necessary

> attribute thereof, even as the rays of the sun are an essential requirement of the sun itself.
>
> This explanation, however brief, is complete. Reflect upon it and, God willing, you will grasp the details.[16]

In *Paris Talks* 'Abdu'l-Bahá explains further how the only movement of the soul is toward perfection:

> Now let us consider the soul. We have seen that movement is essential to existence; nothing that has life is without motion. All creation, whether of the mineral, vegetable or animal kingdom, is compelled to obey the law of motion; it must either ascend or descend. But with the human soul, there is no decline. Its only movement is towards perfection; growth and progress alone constitute the motion of the soul.[17]

And how progress is an expression of the spirit in the world of matter.

> In the world of spirit there is no retrogression. The world of mortality is a world of contradictions, of opposites; motion being compulsory everything must either go forward or retreat. In the realm of spirit there is no retreat possible, all movement is bound to be towards a perfect state. 'Progress' is the expression of spirit in the world of matter. The intelligence of man, his reasoning powers, his knowledge, his scientific achievements, all these being manifestations of the spirit, partake of the inevitable law of spiritual progress and are, therefore, of necessity, immortal.[18]

Practical application of the work of the soul

In answer to a question, 'Abdu'l-Bahá is reported to have said:

> Listen then my children. The human soul is to be compared to a weaver; the human life is the thing woven, the

cloth; the human body, principally the brain, is the tool, the instrument with which the weaving is done.

God the Lord, the Master of the works, prepares the loom, that is the warp for the loom, the human milieu or environment with the ground-threads of fate. Thereby will be forced on the human being, the place, the time, the parents, the religion, nationality, society qualities, that is of gifted persons etc.

The human soul then throws across the warp-threads the filling or woof by means of the shuttle that is the five senses, imagination, action, whereby up to the end of life as we say, are developed the masterpieces of the human life . . .

The materials for weaving may be of hemp-yarn, wool or silk, or some other mixture – which cannot be chosen by the soul, nor can the soul select the tools, but only the pattern and the method of weaving, insofar as it is not already predestined by the material itself to a certain degree. The material represents the inherited, (that is taken over) body organization.[19]

I am a tapestry weaver, so found this description of how the soul 'weaves' our lives fascinating, and I can understand the process being recounted. However, for those less familiar with weaving, here is my personal take on the above:

'Abdu'l-Baha is saying that 'the masterpieces of human life' are the work of the soul. Using the inherited characteristics of the individual as the weft, the soul weaves the weft into the warp of individual circumstances (place, time, parents, religion, nationality, etc.) using imagination, action and the senses. The tools the soul uses are the brain and body of the individual.

In summary

I would humbly suggest that the human spirit or the rational soul, and the human capacities of intelligence, creativity knowledge and skills, are all one! Whether we acknowledge the role of the human spirit or rational soul in our lives or not, the soul is integral to being human, it is what makes us different from the animal. It is the driving force behind the evolving world in which we live. As 'Abdu'l-Bahá suggests, any progress we make in the world of humanity is an expression of the spirit, because man's intelligence, knowledge and powers of reason etc are manifestations of the world of the spirit.

Bahá'u'lláh describes this concept in the *Seven Valleys*:

> 'Increase my wonder and amazement at Thee, O God!'
>
> Likewise, reflect upon the perfection of man's creation, and that all these planes and states are folded up and hidden away within him.
>
> Dost thou deem thyself a small and puny form,
> When thou foldest within thyself the greater world?
>
> We must therefore labour to destroy the animal condition, till the meaning of humanity cometh to light.[20]

However, this raises questions: How do we connect to this understanding? How can we enhance our spiritual and human capacities? What is the relationship between the arts, science, spiritual and human capacities, and education?

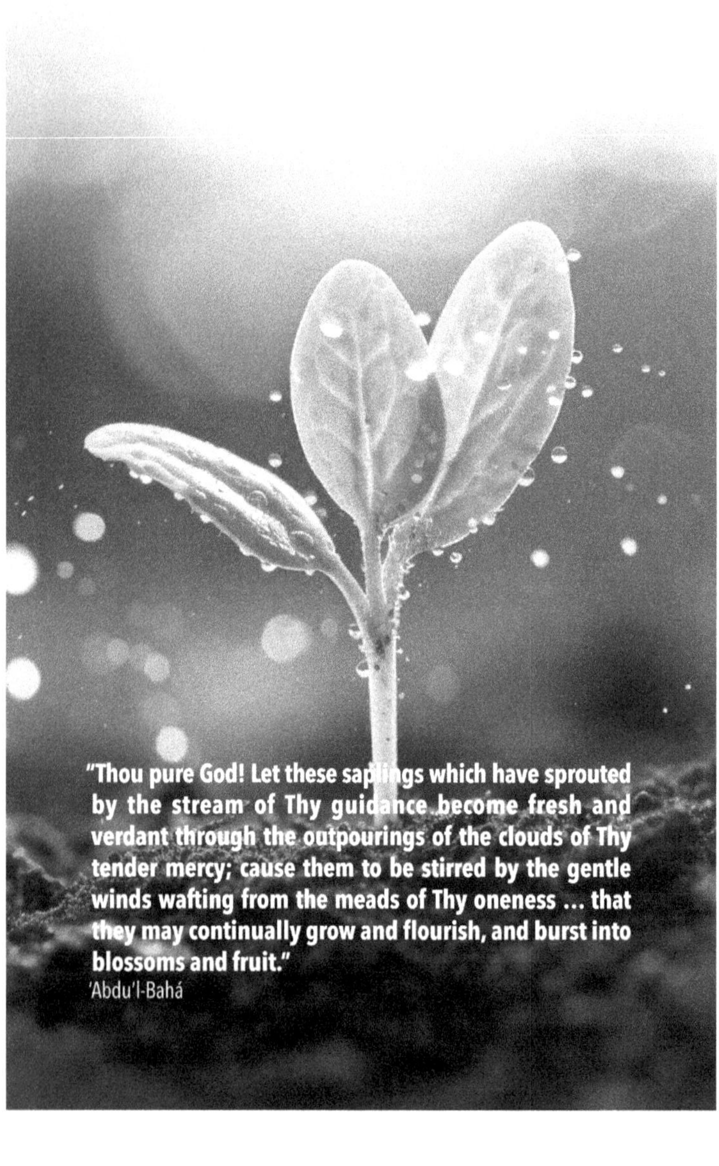
"Thou pure God! Let these saplings which have sprouted by the stream of Thy guidance become fresh and verdant through the outpourings of the clouds of Thy tender mercy; cause them to be stirred by the gentle winds wafting from the meads of Thy oneness … that they may continually grow and flourish, and burst into blossoms and fruit."
'Abdu'l-Bahá

4 Science and Art of Education

Howard Gardner, in thinking about education in this globalized world, says that he believes that current formal education still prepares students primarily for the world of the past, rather than possible worlds of the future. He makes the point that although science is taught, scientific ways of thinking are not, neither are the creative capacities developed that are essential for technological progress. He also asserts that too often we think of science as the prototype of all knowledge, rather than one powerful way of knowing that needs to be complemented by artistic and humanistic and perhaps also spiritual stances.[1]

Robinson and Gardner both agree that we are living in a fast-changing world where the creative industries are leading, yet there is a political insistence on ignoring the evidence and demanding a narrow science-based education that undervalues the creative capacities of the population. The divisions still exist between science and arts because there is, as Robinson points out, a conflation between the notions of 'academic' and 'educational'.

How is education understood?

Education can be broadly defined as:

- receiving or giving systematic instruction
- a body of knowledge acquired while being educated
- training in a particular subject

The word 'education' is derived from the Latin, from the verbs *educare*, which means to train, and *educere*, meaning to draw or lead out. Dictionary definitions point to the general understanding that 'education' is about the 'classroom'. However, as stated in a Royal Society of Arts document, 'Anatomy of Learning':

> It is also important to remember that most of the learning we do in life is neither academic nor school based. Young people all over the world are learning to animate, cook, knit, do magic, skateboard or play the guitar by watching people on YouTube. We prioritise a narrow conception of academic knowledge at our peril. It results in too many young people being cowed and dismissed by school.[2]

This statement points to the danger of seeing 'education' as being about learning facts and information and passing exams. It suggests that as a result of a narrow understanding there are many young people who emerge from education disillusioned and feeling they have failed themselves and their families. This is surely not the fault of the young people; it is the persistent belief that 'academic' means 'educated'. Why is this such an insistent belief?

The education system we now have in the west, with its roots in history, has been influential in many areas of the world, as colonialism took hold and missionaries spread their understanding of education across the world. It has evolved over time and been buffeted by varying political persuasions which each demanded their own 'take' on the educational needs of children. But has it moved on to serve the needs of the 21st century? Has it played a role in creating a perceived division between art and science?

The oldest school in the United Kingdom was founded by St Augustine in Canterbury in 597 AD. The sons of landed gentry were taught Latin grammar and were prepared for work within the church; however, over time those educated in these schools followed a variety of professions, in law, diplomacy, medicine and politics. Grammar schools proliferated, and by the end of the 15th century there were about 300 under the auspices of mainly religious institutions.

In the 1700s, as the rift between science and art deepened, other organizations began to establish their own schools, and the curriculum in the church schools broadened, to be what we would call classical in emphasis, based on the seven liberal arts or sciences. It led to what became known as the classical illusion, where to be educated meant you had to be able to read Homer in the original language.

There were individual schools where enlightened headmasters attempted to broaden the curriculum, for example the head of Merchant Taylors School from 1561 to 1568 introduced the study of English grammar. He also introduced drama, and the school was known for offering music, dance, drawing and multiple sports.

However, in general, attempts to broaden school curricula in Great Britain did not bear fruits until the 1800s, when the growing impact of science and technology and industrialization became apparent, as demonstrated in the great exhibitions of 1851 and 1862.

By the 1900's the British school curriculum had become established into the now familiar hierarchy, with science, technology, mathematics and languages being the most important, while the humanities and arts were considered less so. Did the classical illusion now become the academic illusion?

There were several major government decisions taken over time. In 1840, the Grammar Schools Act shifted control from church to state, and the curriculum broadened considerably, but this applied mainly to boarding schools preparing children for careers in administration and services. Local education authorities were established in 1902, and local taxes raised the funds to pay for schooling for all. Schools for girls were introduced. By 1904, a four-year curriculum was established.

In 1944, the Butler Act introduced education in two tiers, primary for ages 5–11, and secondary for ages 12–15. At the secondary stage there were three options; grammar, secondary modern, and secondary technical. Entrance to a grammar school was by scholarship examination, which became the 11+ exam.

In 1951, national examinations were introduced, the General Certificate of Education 'O' and 'A' Levels. Between 1965 and 1988, the education system went through changes that saw an introduction of a much more child-centred approach.

In 1988, the Baker Act introduced a compulsory National Curriculum consisting of 14 subjects. Compulsory assessments (SATS) were introduced, and schools were ranked through league tables. Schools with declining headcounts would have to improve or shut down. Market forces were to determine the history of education.

Seeing the story laid out over time, it is easy to understand how the present systems have arisen. The original goals of the monastic schools evolved eventually into the tiered system of grammar schools and secondary modern schools of the 1950s. The grammar/secondary modern hierarchy maintained the separation of academic and non-academic as the basis for education, and even when in 1965 there was a move to eliminate the hierarchy through the introduction of the comprehensive structure, the academic/non-academic or science/art divide was maintained.

Ken Robinson, with his passion for education and the importance of creativity for not only personal well-being but economic success, expertly throws light on the sources of the separation of arts and sciences. He points out that young people, in the process of education, are sorted through filters. The first is economic, in that education categorizes people on implicit assumptions about the labour market; while the second is intellectual, sorting people according to a very particular view of intelligence that results in 'the assumption that there are only two types of people . . . academic and non-academic, or as they are often called . . . the able and the less able'.[3]

Schools were established on an 'industrial model' in the 1800s, where the children were fed onto the school 'conveyor belt', and then passed through a curriculum based mainly on academic learning. As they travelled through the system, they would be identified as 'academic and therefore intelligent' or 'vocational and not so intelligent'; over time they were shaped, built, constructed, packed and then stamped as being ready for a specific 'market' such as factory worker, shopkeeper, diplomat, secretary, housemaid, teacher, politician, labourer, farm worker, etc. Education prepared the child for a specific life occupation, decisions about which were determined by the child showing either 'academic' or 'vocational' tendencies.

The 1944 Education Act set up the grammar school, secondary modern school and technical school, with the presumption that the 20 per cent educated in the grammar schools would supply the 'professional' needs of the country by ensuring a rigorous academic education, while the remaining 80 per cent were sent to secondary modern or technical schools and were destined for the 'manual trades', and were given a 'watered down' version of the grammar school curriculum.

Robinson explains that as long as good academic qualifications were gained, and if students also went on to university, then secure lifelong employment was guaranteed. However, the nature of the technological and economic developments in the world now requires different approaches. The economic model on which present assumptions are made has radically changed, in that the economy demands different skills, led in the main by technological advances that have changed the way the world communicates and economies function.

Governments, however, says Robinson, seem to think that the best way of preparing for the massive changes that the future promises is simply to repeat the same system, with more tests, demanding higher academic levels, and utilizing a system where schools that cannot reach these levels are labelled as 'failing'. It is not wrong, of course, to want higher standards, but perhaps the whole purpose of education needs to be revised in the light of present and future needs. Should the desired improvement of the education system be predicated on being 'blamed and shamed' and labelled a failure? Is this really an efficient way to encourage achievement?

In relation to economic needs, Robinson identifies the fastest growing areas of the UK economy as the creative industries – interesting when it is remembered that traditionally the arts (here understood as the visual, performing and written arts) were seen as recreational and leisure-orientated and considered enjoyable and interesting, but not useful.

This raises an important point, because the creative

industries, commonly defined as architecture, TV, radio, film, fashion, media, software, games, advertising, etc., are all areas where the value depends on an ability to generate ideas rather than commodities. They are now a powerful element within economies, but the education systems, still structured around academic/non-academic outcomes, are not producing what these industries need, and with policy makers continuing to demand higher academic standards they confuse academic with educational and qualifications with abilities.

Robinson makes the point that there is a 'breathless rate of change in the 21st century', and what is required is people who are adaptable, flexible and creative and able to cope with and contribute to these changes.

This is about human fulfilment, knowing who you are and what you are as a human being. How many children pass through the education system never knowing who they truly are? – considering themselves failures, not intelligent? and yet in their hearts they yearn to do something, or express themselves in a particular way, that they have never had the opportunity to discover. Being human is about being creative, acknowledging this fact and developing our capacity to utilize this aspect of ourselves.

Ken Robinson in his final book, *Imagine If*, published in 2022 after his death, talks about 'rewilding education'. He states:

> Much like the agricultural systems that thrive when the soil is right, we thrive when the culture is right. An education system is not successful because of tests and output driven hurdles; it is successful when individuals are recognized, and the diversity of their talent is celebrated. It is successful when students are fulfilled to live fulfilling lives.
>
> Education will only truly progress when we understand and recognize that it too is a living system, and that the art is to invigorate the living culture of the schools themselves. Just as skilful farmers focus on the soil to create the conditions for plants to grow and flourish, skilful schools focus

on creating the conditions for children to grow and flourish.[4]

What do the Bahá'í writings suggest as the purpose of education?

Education is of paramount importance within the Bahá'í teachings. It is central to the spiritual and material well-being of mankind.

> Regard man as a mine rich in gems of inestimable value. Education can, alone, cause it to reveal its treasures, and enable mankind to benefit therefrom.[5]

> The Purpose of the one true God, exalted be His glory, in revealing Himself unto men is to lay bare those gems that lie hidden within the mine of their true and inmost selves.[6]

These two quotations from the writings of Bahá'u'lláh are, for me, expressive of the purpose of an education that would enable every child to fulfil their potential. The first one describes mankind as 'mines' full of 'gems' of 'inestimable value', and suggests that education is about mining and revealing those gems, so that they can benefit mankind. What it does not say is that these gems belong to a favoured few! We all have gems, unique to each of us. Their value is totally beyond estimate, and only education, in all its guises, can reveal these gems so that they can benefit mankind. Education here is not about personal careers or material well-being; it is about what each person can contribute to the well-being of humanity by using their unique gems in service to others.

The second quotation then places the process of mining and polishing gems within the larger picture of the whole purpose of the guidance of God. Every individual has 'gems' that are hidden, and not just hidden but buried in the 'mine' of their inmost selves. This analogy is fascinating and perhaps suggests that to discover and bring the gems to the surface we each need the skills and abilities of a 'miner'. The qualities that a miner in the deep mines develops could be, amongst others, tenacity, strength, courage, discipline, determination, respect, daring, confidence. To what extent does the education system give young people the knowledge, tools, skills and qualities they require to mine their gems, bring them to the surface, cut and polish them in readiness to serve humanity? This recalls the concepts of Gardner's multiple intelligences and Robinson's hidden natural resources.

Every child, has, according to this approach, a huge potential. It does not suggest that education should be easy and without challenge, but that it should be an exciting journey of discovery 'in all branches of knowledge, science and the arts'.[7] The Bahá'í perspective suggests that every individual has enormous potential for service to mankind, and that it is only through education and the process of mining and polishing the 'gems' of capacities that this service can be realized. 'Abdu'l-Bahá advised:

> Make every effort to acquire the advanced knowledge of the day, and strain every nerve to carry forward the divine civilization.[8]

> Establish schools that are well organised and promote the fundamentals of instruction in the various branches of knowledge through teachers who are pure and sanctified, distinguished for their high standards of conduct and general excellence, and strong in faith – scholars and educators with a thorough knowledge of sciences and arts . . .
>
> Included must be promotion of the arts, the discovery of new wonders, the expansion of trade, and the development of industry. The methods of civilization and the beautification of the country must also be encouraged . . .[9]

Who then is responsible for enabling these gems to be mined? Is it the teachers? Is it the parents? Is it the government? Is it society as a whole? This brings to mind the words of the Báb:

> Whoever possesseth power over anything must elevate it to its uttermost perfection that it not be deprived of its own paradise.[10]

The teacher possesses power in the classroom, the parent in the home. Is it the teacher's responsibility within the school setting to 'elevate' a child 'to its uttermost perfection that it not be deprived of its own paradise'? Are the parents responsible in the home setting? Are our communities also responsible? In fact, are we all accountable? In one way or another, we all possess power over either ourselves or others as we travel through our lives. 'Abdu'l-Bahá explains:

> O Company of God! To each created thing, the Ancient Sovereignty hath portioned its own perfection, its particular virtue and special excellence, so that each in its degree may become a symbol denoting the sublimity of the true Educator of humankind, and that each, even as a crystalline mirror, may tell of the grace and splendour of the Sun of Truth.[11]

> Exert every effort to acquire the various branches of knowledge and true understanding. Strain every nerve to achieve both material and spiritual accomplishments.
>
> Encourage the children from their earliest years to master every kind of learning, and make them eager to become skilled in every art – the aim being that through the favouring grace of God, the heart of each one may become even as a mirror disclosing the secrets of the universe, penetrating the innermost reality of all things; and that each may earn world-wide fame in all branches of knowledge, science and the arts.
>
> Certainly, certainly, neglect not the education of the children. Rear them to be possessed of spiritual qualities, and be assured of the gifts and favours of the Lord.[12]

Should one of the goals of the education system be to recognize the complexity of both the spiritual and human capacities, together with recognition of the innate capacity of every individual to contribute to the betterment of the world? If everyone emerged from the educational experience having discovered their particular abilities, linked with a passion and desire to offer them in service to the world – in other words finding their 'element' – then surely the world would benefit not only from their accumulated knowledge but also their passion to share, through their skills, that knowledge with others.

In summary

According to the Bahá'í teachings the focus of education is twofold: the first is to reveal the gems hidden within the mines of our inmost selves; the second is to ensure that those gems are brought to the surface, cut and polished, and utilized in service to humanity.

This is a very different aim from present educational systems where, in general, the focus is on academic superiority, being the best, being first in order that the individual might gain the right to the best job, with the most reward.

Equipping individuals to serve by offering their knowledge and skills for the betterment of the world would automatically mean that the long-term view changes. Rather than seeing education as the stepping-stone to personal gain, in wealth, status, and material benefits, the view would be outward-looking, service-orientated. Work would automatically have a different feel, in that whatever work was taken on, it would be considered as service to humanity. True service does not have status, so the purpose of gaining qualifications would have a very different focus, and it would be more important that each individual discovered their true gems and found their element, so that the service could be truly meaningful.

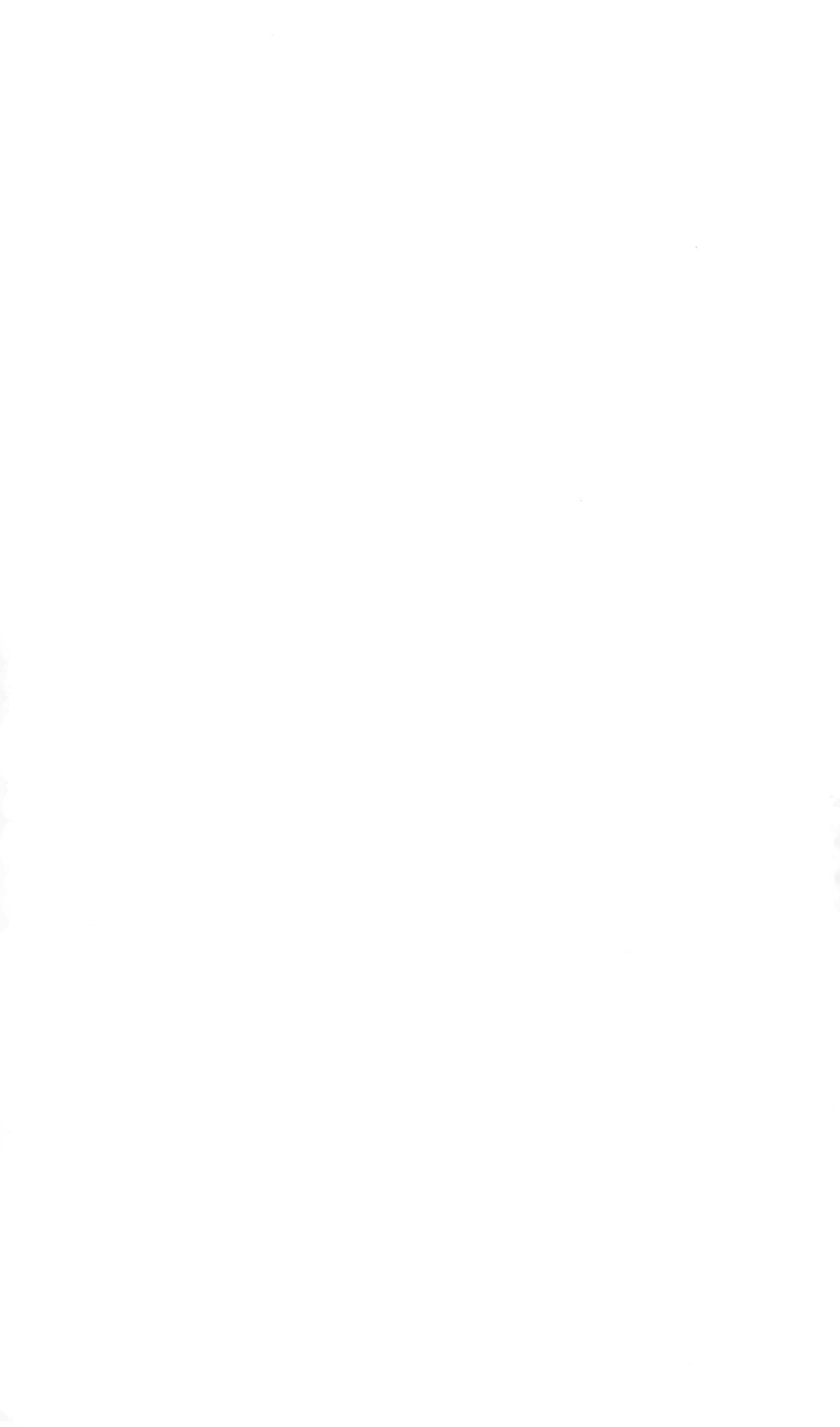

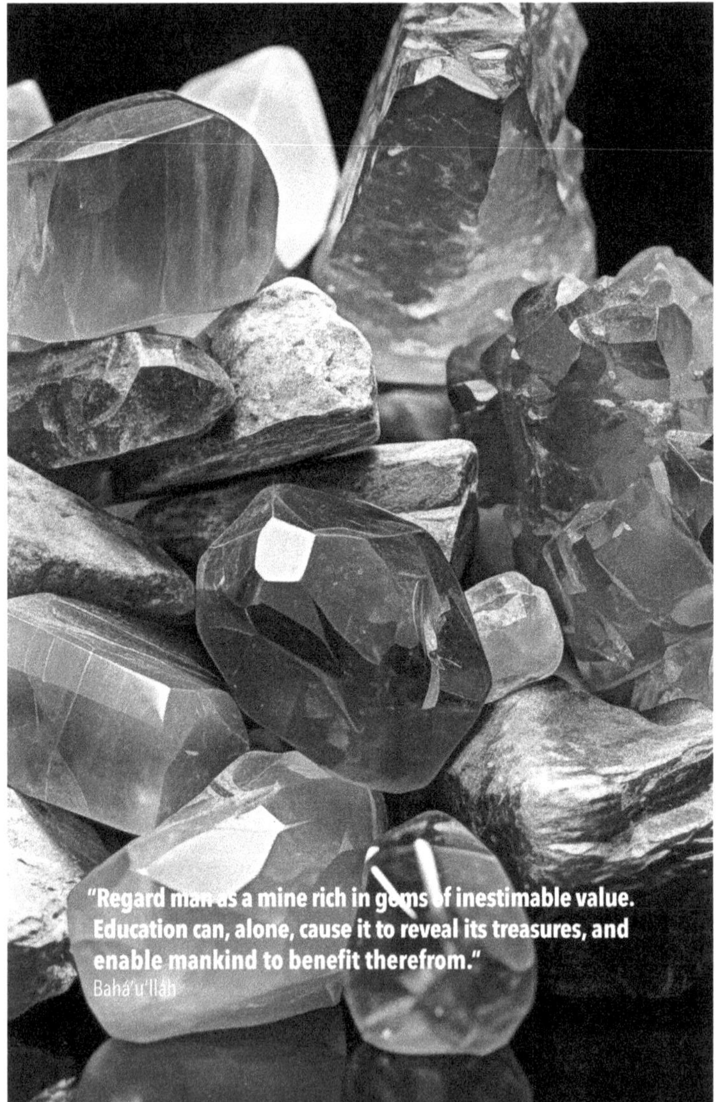
"Regard man as a mine rich in gems of inestimable value.
Education can, alone, cause it to reveal its treasures, and
enable mankind to benefit therefrom."
Bahá'u'lláh

5 Science and Art of Bahá'í Learning Spaces

Every aspect of life is a learning space – at home, at work, at play or enjoying lifetime passions – but some spaces are more structured towards learning than others. Schools and universities are both examples of this. However, within the emerging Bahá'í community the concept of learning is central and crucial to its development. We have a framework for action which places learning and its application at the heart of community life. There is the twofold moral purpose of attending to one's own spiritual and intellectual development and also contributing to the transformation of society by offering our own knowledge and skills, and accompanying others to discover theirs.

This echoes the concepts expressed by 'Abdu'l-Bahá as knowledge, volition and action, or in the words of the Universal House of Justice, the generation, application and diffusion of knowledge.

I would like to explore two spaces which illustrate this learning mode: they are the Ruhi Institute, and Bahá'í summer schools.

Science and art of the Ruhi Institute

The Ruhi Institute, as described in detail below, has been essential in contributing to an evolving and growing world-wide community, where in every village, town, city and neighbourhood, it is proving to be a positive influence in enabling all age groups to recognize how every individual can come to recognize their spiritual identity and, by developing both their own spiritual and material knowledge and understanding, and the skills to apply them within their communities, they can contribute to the progress of the world toward peace and unity.

The Ruhi Institute is described as follows:

> Its purpose is to assist individuals to deepen their understanding of the Bahá'í teachings, and to gain the spiritual insights and practical skills they need to carry out the work of the community.[1]

What is the Ruhi Institute and what is its conceptual framework?

> The Ruhi Institute is an educational institution . . . which dedicates its efforts to the development of human resources for the spiritual, social, and cultural development of the Colombian people . . .its area of influence extends throughout the entire country. Especially in recent years, its educational programs have been adopted by an increasing number of agencies worldwide.

Like any other institution involved in the process of education for development, the Ruhi Institute has formulated its strategies within a particular framework and a philosophy of social change, development and education. In this case, that understanding has emerged from a consistent effort to apply Bahá'í principles to the analysis of social conditions.

The Bahá'í Faith sees the present state of human affairs as a natural stage in an organic process which will finally lead to the unity of the human race within one social order. Humanity as a whole has gone through evolutionary stages similar to those experienced by an individual; having passed through infancy and childhood, it is now experiencing the difficult culminating moments of a turbulent adolescence. The present state of confusion, doubt, and belligerence is simply to be understood as the condition of an adolescent who strongly desires growth and maturity, but is still attached to childish attitudes and customs.

Yet the moment is ripe for this adolescent to take a final step and enter the constructive and dynamic but balanced state of maturity and adulthood.

In analysing the rapid changes occurring in the world today, Bahá'ís identify two parallel processes operating at all levels—village, town, nation, and global society. On the one hand, it is clear that human society is suffering from a process of disintegration that manifests itself in wars, terrorism, chaos, physical and psychological insecurity, and a widespread condition of material poverty. On the other hand, forces of integration are moving individuals and groups toward the adoption of new values, new forms of organization, and appropriate structures that can lay the foundation for the establishment of a new social order. The Ruhi Institute defines its basic aim as that of becoming a channel for the spiritual forces of our time to be applied to the lives of the masses of humanity, empowering them to contribute to the establishment of a new world civilization.[2]

The Universal House of Justice has over the years made many references to knowledge and skills and how important they are to the achievement of the goal of universal peace and prosperity. In 2010 its message to the Bahá'ís of the world at Riḍván stated:

> That the world civilization now on humanity's horizon must achieve a dynamic coherence between the material and spiritual requirements of life is central to the Bahá'í teachings. Clearly this ideal has profound implications for the nature of any social action pursued by Bahá'ís, whatever its scope and range of influence. Though conditions will vary from country to country, and perhaps from cluster to cluster, eliciting from the friends a variety of endeavours, there are certain fundamental concepts that all should bear in mind. One is the centrality of knowledge to social existence. The perpetuation of ignorance is a most grievous form of oppression; it reinforces the many walls of prejudice that stand as barriers to the realization of the oneness

> of humankind, at once the goal and operating principle of Bahá'u'lláh's Revelation. Access to knowledge is the right of every human being, and participation in its generation, application and diffusion a responsibility that all must shoulder in the great enterprise of building a prosperous world civilization—each individual according to his or her talents and abilities. Justice demands universal participation.[3]

In 2021:

> Increasingly, participation in institute courses is preparing the friends of God for an ever-deeper engagement in the life of the wider community; it is endowing them with the knowledge, insights, and skills that enable them to contribute not only to the process of developing their own community, but to the progress of society.[4]

In 2023:

> How different actions look when viewed in light of the society-building power they release! This expansive prospect allows a sustained activity to be seen as much more than an isolated act of service or just a data point. In place after place, the initiatives being pursued reveal a population learning how to take increasing responsibility for navigating the path of its own development. The resulting spiritual and social transformation manifests itself in the life of a people in a variety of ways. In the previous series of Plans, it could be seen most clearly in the promotion of spiritual education and collective worship. In this new series of Plans, increasing attention needs to be given to other processes that seek to enhance the life of a community – for example, by improving public health, protecting the environment, or drawing more effectively on the power of the arts. What is required for all these complementary aspects of a community's well-being to advance is, of course, the

> capacity to engage in systematic learning in all these areas—a capacity that draws on insights arising from the Teachings and the accumulated store of human knowledge generated through scientific enquiry. As this capacity grows, much will be accomplished over the coming decades.[5]

The Ruhi Institute approach is a unique educational process for the spiritual education of all age groups, and is predicated on acquiring knowledge and understanding of spiritual teachings and perfecting the skills required to apply that knowledge and understanding in our own lives, on the international or national stage, in our communities, amongst friends and neighbours, as part of this process of 'building a prosperous world civilization'.

Materials have been evolving over many years, for three age ranges: children from 5 to 11, junior youth from 12 to 14 and adults from 15 years upwards. The same materials are used throughout the world, and it is the responsibility of the teachers, animators and tutors to present these materials appropriately to the respective age groups in their own neighbourhoods.

At all age levels the participants are encouraged to put their learning into action in ways that will benefit their community, using the skills gained in very practical ways, in order that the concept of service to the community becomes integral to the learning.

Creative approaches, or use of the arts to explore and explain deep spiritual concepts, is integral to the process of learning and action in the Ruhi method. However, at the present time, the understanding of 'art' is narrow and confined, particularly in the western parts of the world. It is perceived as being only the visual, performing and written arts. This creates anxiety, because the majority of participants, teachers/animators and tutors do not see themselves as 'artists', and therefore the default position for many is to avoid 'the arts'. Combine that with the experience of the majority within their own education of an academic learning emphasis and the hesitancy is completely understandable.

What would the learning feel like? What would it look like,

if this broader more inclusive understanding of science and art/knowledge and skills were to be applied within the Ruhi process?

Imagine if . . .

The skills or arts that are needed to confidently and efficiently put into practice the vision of the Ruhi Institute, could be seen as linked directly to the knowledge or science of the process. What would this look like?

The following is an attempt to describe this, not in respect of any particular aspect of the Ruhi process, but as a general overview of the approach within this framework.

The science and art of facilitation

The science of facilitation is to know that:

- Every participant, of whatever age group, has huge potential.
- Every group is a combination of unique individuals.
- Every participant will have a unique comfort zone in relation to how they best absorb information and understand concepts presented.

The art is to find ways for every individual:

- To be valued and their potential recognized.
- To feel part of the group, to bond and feel safe.
- To be given opportunities to access the content by recognizing their learning styles or preferences.

One approach is to think of planning the session like composing a piece of music. The most beautiful music has rhythm, moments of pause then activity, quietness and loudness, tonal changes that connect to the heart – in other words it is beautiful because of the variegated pattern of sounds. Translate this into a pattern of activity in a learning session, where there might be moments of:

- ◇ small group discussions
- ◇ individual reflection or study
- ◇ active making and creating
- ◇ physical games and drama
- ◇ reading and consultation in plenary
- ◇ reflection on visual presentations, images, film or animation.
- ◇ serious discussion
- ◇ fun laughter and friendship

Why is this important? Because it caters for a variety of learning styles, allows everyone to enjoy a period that speaks to them, that they might then recall, so reinforcing their learning.

It might be thought that this approach is only relevant to children and junior youth, but adults also need variety and rhythm and changes of approach in order to hold their interest and speak to their particular intelligences.

The science and art of planning and organization

The science of planning and organization is to understand the need for being systematic, structured and consistent in attention to the details of the session. To be the composer and conductor of the musical arrangement, and so be in control of the quality of the experience for the learners.

- The art is to put this knowledge into practice consistently, to perfect the skills required and to model an approach that will enthuse and excite the participants.

What might you consider as you plan?

- The content and the concepts behind the content . . . Be sure that you have understood them, because only then can you lift the words off the page and make them come alive for the age group with whom you are working.
- The words on the page will only come alive and be mean-

ingful if you can translate them for the needs of your particular group. Just reading the words does not mean learning is happening, no matter what the age.
- Think how you might convey the concepts/content creatively in a variety of ways to excite and inspire all intelligences and learning styles.
- Do a practice run of all activities planned so that you are aware of the time it might take to complete them, always adding on extra time!
- Plan and record each session, so that you have not only a record of what you have done, but also a resource to reference and to help others achieve the skills of careful planning.

The science and art of empowerment

The science is to know that every human being has potential gems that are unique and of value in building a prosperous world civilization. These gems may be in a multitude of different areas of knowledge and skills . . . maths, engineering, parenting, design, cooking, gardening . . . Every one of these skills can be utilized to inspire and motivate others to learn.

- The art is to find a way to empower each participant to recognize and develop their own gems. This is only going to happen by knowing your participants and constant encouragement to try new experiences.
- The art is using the skills within the group to inspire and motivate, and provide a new learning experience for the group and beyond that in the community.

The science is to know that every learner is on a unique personal journey and should not be judged, compared or criticized in relation to others.

- The art is to always focus on the positive effort and results and ensure that every learner understands that they are on a unique personal journey. This will result in an environment of mutual encouragement where there is no place for competition.

The science is to know that a powerful teaching/animating tool is to keep everyone on the edge of their learning.

- The art is to offer constant loving encouragement to each individual to achieve their best possible result, and then to lead them to the vision of the next goal. Think of the example of the Universal House of Justice in their communications to the Bahá'í world.

The science and art of excellence

The science is to know that everyone can strive for their personal best: 'not beyond that, but not less than that either,' in the words of the Báb.[6]

- The art is to model this excellence in not only the planning but also the delivery of the sessions/classes and encourage everyone to strive for their personal best in whatever is being explored or created.

The science and art of discipline

The science is to understand that discipline is about self- and mutual respect; it is about maximizing learning. When everyone shares that mindset, then activities, games and conversations become a joy, and a process of sharing knowledge and skills. In the context of younger learners, experience demonstrates that although they might 'kick against the rules' they are happier and more confident with boundaries, which provide an environment of safety and security.

- The art is to have endless amounts of love and patience in developing the capacity to be disciplined. True discipline arises from love and respect for each other, the feeling that you do not want to disappoint, cause a problem, etc.

The science is to know why discipline is important to learning, and to understand the context of every situation and accept its limitations.

- The art is to know that as a teacher, animator or tutor you have a role to play in being the 'leader'.

The science and art of creativity

The science is to know and understand that creativity, a function of intelligence, is a natural capacity in everyone, although not everyone recognizes that.

- The art is that the tutor /animator/teacher develops their own capacity to be creative; to open yourself to creative experiences and remember that skills can be learned and then that capacity can be used to encourage others to explore their own creativity.

The science is to know that creativity is expressed through both experiences and objects.

- The art is to offer the opportunity to experience the creative process through every aspect of the planning and delivery of the sessions.
- The art is to also offer the experience of making and fashioning of objects that both enhance learning and deepen understanding.

The science and art of 'art as a learning tool'

The science is to recognize that, rather than being entertainment, the arts or skills are serious and purposeful learning tools to enhance and disseminate knowledge, to consolidate understanding as well as to generate joy, and to strengthen bonds of unity.

- The art is to utilize the creative energy of making, fashioning, enquiring, playing, thinking, questioning, consulting, discussing through a wide variety of media and processes with the aim of enhancing the comprehension of complex concepts and ideas.

The arts or skills of making, fashioning and creating

There is the science and art of tutoring, animating and teaching, but there are also the arts or skills used within that framework to make, fashion, create. These skills require media and at least the basic techniques to become reality. Book 7 of the Ruhi materials addresses this aspect as follows:

> Artistic expression includes a vast area of human endeavour referred to as crafts. Here, scores of materials – leather, wool, cotton, silk, stone, clay, glass, metal, wood, wax, straw, dried flowers, and so on, and so on – are transformed in myriad ways by the skilful hands of craftsmen into objects, both practical and not, taming the inherent qualities of the materials to create beauty.
>
> Remember that we do not consider this an extracurricular activity, but an important element in the methodology of study employed by the Institute. To develop the ability to work with one's hands is not a secondary educational objective. It is an imperative in the overall training of an individual.[7]

And it further states:

> As you have surely gathered from your study of this unit, the task being asked of you does not require you to be an accomplished artist. You need not be an actor, a playwright,

> a poet or a musician to promote the arts at the grassroots level. Nor is a study circle the occasion to prepare individuals for earning a livelihood through arts and crafts. What you need to remember is that the Institute is fundamentally concerned with spiritual and moral empowerment. Exposing its students to various forms of artistic expression constitutes one element in this process. By being a promoter of arts and crafts at the grassroots in ways that have been described in this unit, you will be opening up creative channels through which can flow inspiration and the force of attraction to beauty.[8]

These media and techniques might include:

Media	**Techniques**
Paper & card	Folding, origami, building structures, collage
Film	Photography / video / animation
Modelling materials	3D Modelling, relief modelling,
Ink	Printing, painting, drawing, calligraphy
Pencils, graphite and coloured pencils	Drawing, colouring, creating visual images in any format
Paint	Painting /printmaking/ fabric printing
Wood	Carving / building / making
Plants and natural found objects	Planting / collage /building

Food	Cooking / eating/ entertaining
Words	Writing / poetry / stories / drama scripts
Recycled materials	Collage /sculpture,
The body	Dance / drama / games/ sports / storytelling
Dyes	Dyeing fabric – batik, tie dye
Fibres	Weaving / sewing / macramé / basketry /rugs
Sounds	Instruments / singing / creating songs / writing music

The science and art of learning spaces

Book 7 of the Ruhi materials states:

> One important factor will be the physical environment in which the group meets. Unfortunately, in today's world, physical beauty is often associated with wealth. But a lavish setting is not what is required. There is beauty in nature, in orderliness, in tidiness. You will want to make sure that the environment in which your group studies is one that satisfies the individual's yearning for beauty and perfection, whether the group is sitting under the shade of a tree or gathering in an expensively decorated living room, a humble hut or an institute facility.[9]

The science is to understand the importance of the learning environment to the quality of learning that takes place.

- The art is to utilize whatever is available to make sure the space is orderly, clean, beautiful and appropriate for the learners.
- The art is to create a space that inspires and brings joy to the hearts of participants.

Every art or skill requires practice to develop confidence and expertise with a variety of media, and it is not possible to be expert in all of them, but we are expected only to do our best and then use the skills of the participants, particularly within the older age groups where their capacities can be shared for all to benefit.

Whether tutoring, teaching or animating, the art of planning and organization is central. The art of conversation, the art of making and creating, etc, all require time and effort to attain. If these are new fields of endeavour then they will also require courage and determination to make that effort.

Science and art of summer schools

Another feature of the Bahá'í community is the gathering together of Bahá'ís and their friends over a short period of time in a structured, often residential space, to share learning and devotional programmes and to have time to create bonds of friendship through being together. The aim is to acquire the knowledge and perfect the skills to build prosperous, peaceful and united communities in our own neighbourhoods, towns and cities around the world.

The summer schools in the United Kingdom have been running since 1936! As to be expected they have always been overwhelmingly left-brained or academic-oriented learning events. The 'arts', understood in this historical context as music, dance, drama, etc., were the 'icing on the cake' – a drama or music performance in the evening, or as part of afternoon workshops, the occasional musical interlude to lighten the 'real and serious learning'. Yet as the years went by, we were increasingly being encouraged to use the 'arts', but we did not really understand how to do that without depending entirely on the few 'creative individuals', the 'artists', who could sing, dance, act or play an instrument, etc.

Shoghi Effendi, as Guardian of the Bahá'í Faith, wrote about his vision for summer schools in his many letters to the evolving Bahá'í community. The following extracts give a flavour of these communications.

> Remembering the strong emphasis repeatedly laid by the Guardian on the importance of the institutions of the summer school, both as a centre for the preparation and training of prospective teachers and pioneers, and for the commingling and fellowship of various elements in the Bahá'í community, the Bahá'í Youth . . . have a peculiar responsibility to shoulder in connection with its development into that ideal Bahá'í University of the future, which should be the aim of every existing Bahá'í Summer School to establish in the fullness of time.[10]

> He was very happy to hear of the success of the school, especially that it has been the means of bringing to light hitherto unsuspected capacities among the friends . . . The Summer School has been carrying on the divine work of bringing forth jewels from the mine of humanity and it is the hope of Shoghi Effendi and the friends here that those who have been trained in the Summer School will carry on the work in the various localities from which they have come . . .[11]

> The Guardian cherishes the hope that at the termination of your school this summer every one of the attendants will have derived such mental and spiritual benefits, and acquired such a fresh enthusiasm to serve as will enable him, upon his return to his local community, to labour with a determination and vigour that will excite the envy and admiration of his fellow-believers, and stimulate them to greater heights of consecration to the service of our beloved Cause.[12]

> Shoghi Effendi hopes that your summer school will increasingly develop and will become an important centre for the spread of the Message. You should try to raise its intellectual as well as its spiritual standard and to pave the way for its future development into one of the foremost Bahá'í universities in the West. Much stress should be laid on the thorough study of the history and of the teachings of the Cause, and particularly of the nature, basis and outstanding features of the Administration . . .[13]

The following are points gleaned from *God Passes By* to identify what the Guardian saw as important aspects of summer schools. He wrote: 'Equally important as a factor in the evolution of the Administrative Order has been the remarkable progress achieved . . . by the institution of the summer schools.' These schools, he said, are designed to:

- ◊ foster the spirit of fellowship in a distinctly Bahá'í atmosphere
- ◊ afford the necessary training for Bahá'í teachers
- ◊ provide facilities for the study of the history and teachings of the Faith, and for
- ◊ a better understanding of its relation to other religions and to human society in general

Among the themes to be covered by summer schools are:

- ◊ intensive study of Bahá'í Scriptures and of the early history of the Faith
- ◊ teachings and history of Islam
- ◊ the promotion of inter-racial amity
- ◊ the processes of the Bahá'í Administrative Order
- ◊ special sessions devoted to youth and child training
- ◊ classes in public speaking
- ◊ comparative religion
- ◊ the manifold aspects of the Faith (group disccussions)

- ◇ Bahá'í ethics
- ◇ forums and devotional gatherings
- ◇ plays and pageants
- ◇ picnics and other recreational activities

Summer schools are to be:

- ◇ open to Bahá'ís and non-Bahá'ís alike, and
- ◇ to evolve into the Bahá'í universities of the future.[14]

Everything that has been shared earlier in this chapter in terms of the sciences and arts of planning and organization, facilitation of learning, excellence, empowerment, and so on, are all relevant to the delivery of a summer school. However, perhaps the overriding science and art is that of a creative approach to planning and organization.

United vision

For residential schools to succeed there must firstly be a united vision, a vision that everyone responsible totally believes in. Where does this vision emerge from? It is most successful if it comes from the guidance of the Bahá'í institutions in consultation with the organizing team. My experience has shown me that it is important for the team to 'own' the vision, embrace it as their own, so that the school becomes their 'baby', and they have a personal investment in making it happen to the best of their ability.

Adequate time to plan

Long experience shows that the most productive time scale is that as soon as one event has finished, the process of reflection and evaluation leads immediately to planning for the next event. In this way the planning of courses and activities can be completed, and individuals being asked to take on responsibilities within the school can be given good notice to allow them to think through, consult and plan their role.

Attention to detail

Anyone who has visited the Bahá'í World Centre in Haifa as a pilgrim, or served there in any capacity, will have experienced the attention to detail of planning. This is the ultimate model to follow.

In Haifa the starting point for pilgrimage is love for the pilgrims: they are honoured guests, so their every comfort is thought through and attended to. There is a sense that the staff are simply there to serve their needs. This is how it should be for summer school.

Communications should be loving, warm, clear and precise, and in good time; programmes exciting and inspiring for all ages – in other words, the aim is to create a school that will be unforgettable. As Shoghi Effendi says, the outcome should be that everyone returns home having 'derived such mental and spiritual benefits' and having 'acquired such fresh enthusiasm to serve' that he will 'excite the envy and admiration' of his fellow believers and inspire them to greater heights of service.

In order for this wish of Shoghi Effendi to be fulfilled, one aspect of the process that could be considered important is how the courses are described, so that participants when selecting a course are able to make a considered choice in relation to their particular learning style. For this to happen, the course descriptions need to describe both the content/themes of the course and the delivery style of the tutor. In other words, both the science and art, the knowledge and skills are clear. The tutor might list/describe briefly the content or subject matter of the course, but also say clearly how it will be delivered. For example:

- This course will explore the themes through mainly text-based material, with ample opportunity for meaningful discussion and conversation. Extensive notes will be supplied for study and reference.
- The content of this course will be explored through a combination of visual presentations, active participation

in group tasks, and individual tasks, allowing ample time for conversation and discussion.

These two descriptions inform the participants of the learning processes being adopted by the tutor, and from this they can make a considered choice of which course to follow. This is important to ensure that precious time is not lost during the few days of the school, and frustrations do not develop around making the wrong choice.

Planning of the structure and content

The structure and content of a summer school programme will, of course vary from country to country, but wherever the school is, Shoghi Effendi identified three overarching aspects of summer schools: study, devotions and fellowship, apart from all the advice given above.

Think about the balance of all these elements for all age groups. Think of the vision that one day these summer schools, where they have dedicated premises, might become the universities of the future. However, beware lest the concept of universities as they are now trap you into thinking that is the model.

The arts, understood here as the skills perfected to apply knowledge, should permeate the summer school, from the approach to planning and administration, the preparation of an inspiring programme of courses, the facilitators chosen to create and deliver them, the planning of menus to ensure the well-being of participants and the creation of activities to promote friendship and fellowship. This includes, of course, all those traditional arts with which we are so familiar, but with the thinking extended to include all the skills that together create an event that will never be forgotten because of the love demonstrated and the creative skills applied to every detail of the event.

As we have seen earlier in this chapter, the Universal House of Justice in 2023 called on the Bahá'í community to draw more effectively on the power of the arts, and equal with attention to be given to public health and the environment. We might draw from this that the arts /skills are equally important as these other areas of learning, but it demands that we develop the capacity to:

> . . . engage in systematic learning in all these areas – a capacity that draws on insights arising from the Teachings and the accumulated store of human knowledge generated through scientific enquiry. As this capacity grows, much will be accomplished over the coming decades.[15]

In summary

Might the quality of Bahá'í learning environments, whether a residential event for the Ruhi books, or a summer school, or small group study circles, be improved if every organizer, tutor, animator, teacher or facilitator acquired the knowledge and skills, together with the confidence to apply them in practice? I would say, from my own experience as participant, organizer and facilitator over many years – a resounding yes!

We are intelligent creative beings and we can acquire any knowledge and perfect any skill we wish to. We are limited only by our own volition and time.

Like growing crops, education is an organic process; it requires a rich soil to ensure that all the nutrients are present to nurture the learning and progress of every individual. In the case of education, this soil is made up of love, acceptance, respect and humility. This rich soil must be fed with encouragement and challenge, enthusiasm, stimulation and motivation. Learners must be engaged and inspired to be active agents of their own growth, ready to participate and then take their learning out and use it in the service of others.

All the above implies that, with creative thinking and doing in the designing, planning and delivery of learning, the desired outcomes will be easier to achieve, and will enhance and disseminate knowledge and consolidate understanding, as well as generate joy and strengthen bonds of unity.

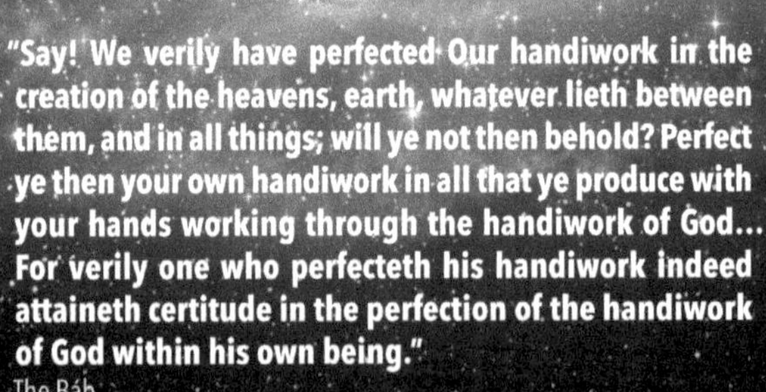
"Say! We verily have perfected Our handiwork in the creation of the heavens, earth, whatever lieth between them, and in all things; will ye not then behold? Perfect ye then your own handiwork in all that ye produce with your hands working through the handiwork of God... For verily one who perfecteth his handiwork indeed attaineth certitude in the perfection of the handiwork of God within his own being."
The Báb

6 Science and Art of Life

Considered from the perspective offered in this book, there is nothing that we do in this world that does not require the acquisition of knowledge and the perfection of skills; therefore, we can say that science and art permeate every aspect of all our lives.

How might these concepts apply to our lives?

As soon as the concept of the integration and connectedness of science and art is accepted, we can approach everything we do in a more holistic manner. Immediately, there is a natural necessity for us all to extend our knowledge of all the complex components we need to make the best of our lives and develop the skills and confidence, using our intelligences and creativity, to apply our knowledge and provide the best for our loved ones and the world we inhabit.

There is a realization that, as the Universal House of Justice said, we are **all** responsible for the acquisition, the application and the diffusion of knowledge, according to our unique capacities. That, whatever our profession, occupation, our role in life, this applies to every aspect of our lives: working, playing, educating, studying, parenting. Our unique combination of knowledge and skills can contribute to the great enterprise of building a prosperous world civilization.

How does this concept play out in the lives of real people?

The following individuals were asked to share how they thought their sciences and arts contribute to building a prosperous world civilization.

Craftsmanship as spiritual practice

by Philip Koomen FRSA

Craftspeople were considered an anachronism in the 1970s, but not now. Over the last forty years I have trained over twenty people, many of whom have now established their own workshops and are training others. The crafts offer a rewarding livelihood for those who are willing to commit to a life-time of learning. Craftsmanship in its purest and noblest form can be a spiritual practice.

The Báb's and Bahá'u'lláh's teachings offer an unprecedented spiritual manifesto for artists and craftspeople, a guide that will inspire and direct them for generations. Bahá'u'lláh writes:

> Immerse yourselves in the ocean of My words, that ye may unravel its secrets, and discover all the pearls of wisdom that lie hid in its depths.[1]

Craftsmanship in the 21st century

Craftsmanship is the pursuit of excellence for its own sake. According to the eminent sociologist Richard Sennett, craftsmanship is a universal work ethic. A doctor, a parent, a painter, is a craftsperson when their practice is dedicated to doing something well for its own sake. When I began, aged 21, I had no particular skills or obvious talent for design but I was fascinated by the idea of how I could combine furniture design and making with earning a living; this was my goal. My confidence was sustained through Bahá'u'lláh's vision of an unfolding civilization based on humanity's oneness and inherent spirituality. The role of artists and craftspeople is assured in this vision:

> . . . the true worth of artists and craftsmen should be appreciated, for they advance the affairs of mankind.[2]

Despite the challenges, making a living as a craftsperson is a form of spiritual detachment, according to Bahá'u'lláh. Practising detachment in the Bahá'í Faith does not mean divorcing oneself from the world but practising one's craft as a livelihood and for the greater good:

> The best of men are they that earn a livelihood by their calling and spend upon themselves and upon their kindred for the love of God, the Lord of all worlds.[3]

An independent craftsperson striving for excellence can therefore be pursuing a spiritual practice.

The myth of talent

Many people feel unqualified for a creative life because they assume they lack the necessary talent. Bahá'u'lláh empowers all of us to see ourselves as spiritual beings with talents and qualities – 'a mine rich in gems of inestimable value'.[4] Practice is the real secret to progress and discovering our gems. The psychologist Prof Erik Johansson, a pioneer in the science of expertise, shows that what we perceive as innate talent in others is the result of sustained practice over many years. In one of his earliest studies the difference between a competent violinist and a virtuoso was twice the practice, a difference of 3,500 hours, and that was amongst student musicians. In thirty years of research he found the only measurable indicator of accomplishment was practice. Just as the making of my furniture requires hours of sanding and polishing, these gems also require refining and polishing to reveal their potential and beauty. The creative act then becomes a twofold process: as we develop and refine our creative practice we also act on ourselves, becoming better versions of ourselves.

Conscientiousness

The one special quality needed to become a craftsperson, in my experience, is conscientiousness. It is an internal compass, directing and sustaining both the aspiring and master craftsperson in their efforts. A conscientious craftsperson pursuing excellence as an end itself, and guided by self-knowledge, will eventually become an accomplished craftsperson:

> Truthfulness is the foundation of all human virtues. Without truthfulness progress and success, in all the worlds of God, are impossible for any soul.[5]

A conscientious craftsperson is also transforming themselves:

The inner life

One's inner spiritual life requires the same commitment as one's outer creative life if progress is to be sustained over a lifetime; conscientiousness needs to be cultivated. In accordance with Bahá'u'lláh's teachings I begin every day with a devotional and meditative practice. This act is like polishing the mirror of one's heart. It helps remove the 'dust' of worldly preoccupations and protects one from disillusionment and cynicism. It is an act of humility and spiritual refocusing, a preparation for the day's work. Every day is a new beginning:

> A pure heart is as a mirror; cleanse it with the burnish of love and severance from all save God, that the true sun may shine therein and the eternal morning dawn.[6]

The workshop as a sacred space

> Blessed is the spot and the house, and the place . . . and the heart . . . where mention of God hath been made, and His praise glorified.[7]

Since 2018 I have worked on my own, having spent over three decades managing a team of craftspeople. I now enjoy working in solitude with few distractions, and can experience the joy of making as a mindful endeavour. I have become increasingly conscious that my workshop is a sacred space. The work is the same but I have a different approach – I am the maker now. Every commission is a sacred act, a reciprocated trust. I enter a relationship with a client in which we begin a co-creative process through a series of conversations that will guide me, eventually, to an idea that is then translated into a piece of furniture I design and make. My workshop has produced over 1,800 commissions, from a special chopping board for a wedding present that took a few hours to make to a commission for choir stalls that took 2,000 hours. Each commission tells a unique story. The Bahá'í teachings have elevated art and craft done in the spirit of selfless service for the betterment of the world to the station of worship.

> The more thou strivest to perfect it, the closer wilt thou come to God. What bestowal could be greater than this, that one's art should be even as the act of worshipping the Lord?[8]

However, my workshop is not always an oasis of serenity and can be a place of frenetic activity, of frustration, a disaster area, even despair. A craftsperson's relationship with his/her material is a conversation at best but can also be a fight! Creating beautiful things can be fraught with challenges.

Beauty

While we can all appreciate the beauty inherent in nature, nature's resources are extracted, commodified and marketized with little reverence for their sacredness. By contrast, the Bahá'í teachings offer a profound insight into the spiritual significance of materials. According to the Báb, every material thing in the world not only has an energy, a spirit, but also aspires to manifest its highest form of perfection. A stone, for example, aspires to be a ruby, a piece of paper aspires to have beautiful calligraphy written on it – and so it is with wood, metal, paint, and so on. It therefore becomes a spiritual act when the craftsperson creates objects that represent the highest level of refinement that they can achieve: 'For every thing within its own limits desires to attain to the highest point of its limits'.[9]

The Báb describes this practice as a spiritual obligation, an act of conscientiousness, and true self-mastery: 'For verily one who perfecteth his handiwork indeed attaineth certitude in the perfection of the handiwork of God within his own being'.[10] This teaching, which has recently been translated, has awakened a new sensibility in me and has had a profound influence on my own practice; even after forty years of practice there is more to learn.

The role of craftsmanship in a world civilization

As humanity searches for a direction, a purpose, a new form of craftsperson is already emerging, one who is striving to live a holistic life through applying the intelligences of the body, mind and spirit to create new forms that reflect their spiritual attributes and vision. Craftsmanship can not only be a process of material transformation but a process in which the craftsperson and ultimately society are transformed.

> The source of crafts, sciences and arts is the power of reflection. Make ye every effort that out of this ideal mine there may gleam forth such pearls of wisdom and utterance as will promote the well-being and harmony of all the kindreds of the earth.[11]

What a piece of work is man! or the divine art of living

by Beverley Matthews

Every day I recite a prayer in which I bear witness to a belief that God has created me so I may 'know and worship' Him. It's a bewildering concept: how can we ever know God? That said, a part of me understands on some level – like sitting in a darkened theatre and understanding a Shakespeare play even though I don't totally understand the nuances of the language verbatim. I hear it on one level, yet there's some form of osmosis going on.

I haven't always recited daily prayers. I grew up in a home that eschewed religion. My mother had been raised a Catholic, the hell, fire and brimstone kind, and was psychologically burnt; my father, once released from the Jesuit boarding school where he spent his entire childhood and teen years, often found the outside world a hypocritical place, particularly when it came to religion. So, by the time I came along, my parents were 'done with religion'.

Home life was often chaotic and full of drama and I learned from an early age to cope with uncertainty. I turned to the natural world for connection and, living in Canada, a veritable outdoor cathedral, I would spend many childhood hours playing in the woods feeling at one with the cycle of the seasons, at one with my own sense of God. Blazing summers gave way to fluorescent autumns that slid into wintry snowstorms; drama surrounded me, both outdoors and at home. It's no wonder that later in life I landed on the stage, taking a career as an actor. In childhood I created a ritual to anchor myself, which I've kept to this day: at night I would search the sky for 'my star' and 'pray' to it. It gave me conversation with God.

Whatever our childhood conditions, our parents and caregivers pass on knowledge and skills (and genetics) that become the stuff from which our characters emerge. My mother was a people-person and possessed a huge heart of loving-kindness for all whom she met. She was also creative and spiritually perceptive. My father was an extremely discerning, deep thinker filled with wonder. When I left home after high school, I carried this backpack of inherited knowledge and skills along with me. I was fearless and travelled widely with resilience and courage. Those skills and the knowledge acquired put me in good stead socially, I formed friendships easily and developed many deep and enduring relationships. For years I made a living as a waitress, barmaid, barista and cook in several countries, serving more hot meals throughout those years than I think I've eaten in my lifetime.

In my late twenties I heard about the Bahá'í Faith (through my parents!) and was attracted to its principle of 'unfettered personal investigation of truth' (no clergy, perfect!). For me it was an intriguing system that offered a prescription for living focused on divine principles, and it reframed the purpose of religion. It also gave a fascinating historical perspective on civilization and its unfoldment, and an actual language to enhance the silent conversation I had been having with God. The Bahá'í writings and prayers shed light on the purpose of religion, its society-building powers, and I resonated with its concept of oneness and its main aim of unity. I also loved the principle that science and religion need to be in harmony.

> Dost thou deem thyself a small and puny form,
> When thou foldest within thyself the greater world?[12]

Wandering the globe, developing relationships, and becoming more and more curious about spiritual matters, all this became the perfect preparation for drama school. It was timely to train my body and mind, to take on a formal study, even without a particular end-goal in sight. An actor's training calls one to subtle disciplines of mind and spirit: it offers up a whole new vocabulary of the senses, widens spatial awareness, opens potential to acquire refined mechanics of speech, becomes a portal of creativity through which one can express ideas, impulse and desire, and it emphasizes the importance of choice and intention. One especially enlightening outcome from my training was the discovery of how an actor attunes to 'the space between', that mysterious place where performer and audience commingle and connect. And while these techniques are the arsenal of an actor's craft, research continues on phenomena such as entrainment (where audience heartbeats synchronize with those of the performers during the collective experience), and today these heightened sensibilities and refined perceptions are referred to as 'new science'. Studies continue to examine how sound vibrations influence humans and other life forms, how intention behind spoken words can have profound impact and outcome, including the power of prayer.

Illumine my inner being, O my Lord,
with the splendours of the Dayspring of Thy Revelation,
even as Thou didst illumine my outer being
with the morning light of Thy favour.[13]

Later I moved into screenwriting, a natural complement to acting and another useful creative tool. Even greater opportunity to widen my skillset and knowledge then came when I married and became a mother. The experiences gained throughout those major life-stages offered new insights on the drama of my own childhood and boosted my creative powers to process it. My written and performed work became more mature as renewed perspectives called me to empathy, compassion, and patience. As I learned to co-create a peaceful family home and raise a healthy child alongside my husband, my domestic life and personal growth were also enhanced by being part of a vibrant Bahá'í community. My skills and knowledge as a performer and writer merged seamlessly with day-to-day activity as I strove to improve my loving relationships.

As with acting, the importance of intention took on greater importance and I consciously called on more and more creativity to enhance my engagements, and because Bahá'ís consider acts of service as akin to worship, I acquired more and more skills and knowledge in spaces that focused on community building. In terms of professional work, I found myself choosing only projects where unity and oneness was at the heart.

> . . . the purpose for which mortal men have,
> from utter nothingness,
> stepped into the realm of being,
> is that they may work for the betterment of the world
> and live together in concord and harmony.[14]

To be human is to search for meaning. Conscious or not, we are all questing to understand our unique purpose in life. We seek truth and beauty. If we are taught methods to become cognizant of our unique skills and knowledge, to honour them, and bear witness to their purpose and meaning in our lives, can this process be considered an art? I believe so, for it is in this very considered place that transformation can flourish, both personally and societally. The more curious we become about the knowing and the worshipping, and combine that with a yearning to work for the betterment of society, we naturally become more conscious and outward-looking. Narrow, self-centred modes of operation naturally give way to patterns of oneness and unity.

> Regard man as a mine rich in gems of inestimable value.
> Education can, alone, cause it to reveal its treasures,
> and enable mankind to benefit therefrom.[15]

Today I am aware of daily opportunities to employ my arts. In all the roles I play – mother, daughter, friend, actor, writer, seeker, servant, neighbour, curious creative – there are many spaces calling me to meaningful conversations and practical actions, each opportunity bringing depth to my purpose. And I remain ever-conscious of 'the space between', that mystical place discovered in drama school, where connection and a reciprocity take place. My actions, the choices I make, are my prayers, they are my conversation with God. And they are an essential accompaniment to the written prayer I recite every day, the one in which I seek to 'know and worship' God. The more I worship, the more I know, the more I know, the more I feel drawn to worship. Nature itself is all about cycles, in all its dramatic beauty.

What a piece of work is man!
How noble in reason, how infinite in faculty!
In form and moving how express and admirable!
In action how like an angel,
in apprehension how like a god![16]

The science and art of data analysis

by Dr Hamish McPharlin

I have one of those jobs that didn't exist 20 years ago.

I am the Head of Content Insight at CNN; what this means is that I measure and try to understand who comes to CNN.com; how they got there, what they want to read or watch, and whether our audience tastes change over time. I do this for two stakeholders: editors, who want to know what to write about; and the sales team, who want to convince potential sponsors that we have an audience with the composition and preferences that match their target audience.

I am essentially a 'data analyst', and if anyone was asked to define whether my work is a 'science' or an 'art' they would invariably say it is a science: the science of mathematics, essentially, as most of my work is running data queries, and running calculations from the output to determine what the data is telling us about the audience. However, over time I have come to the realization that this assumption is actually not at all accurate.

I have worked in this industry for 15 years, and have in that time risen from a junior researcher to head of a global team. This process over time has caused me to think about what particular parts of my skillset have led me to rise up the ranks from a team member to a team leader. The latter of course means that not only must I understand the core skills required, like any analyst, but also train the team, set the vision for what we want to accomplish, and represent the voice of the team to other parts of the business. When I think about what parts of my skills are required for that higher-level function, it is the extent to which I develop two skills: the ability to understand what types of insight will be genuinely useful and actionable for the business, and the ability to present that insight to the business in a succinct and compelling way.

This means developing the ability to craft my message. These days I spend a lot more time than I used to thinking about how to present my data. Where, previously, I may have produced a simple bar chart and a brief statement explaining what is going on, I now go over and over the styling and wording. I change the chart type, add colours, remove things that distract from the point I'm trying to make, change the words, and so on. I focus and focus the chart until it is exactly communicating the point. My charts these days are much simpler than they used to be, but they take much more time, because arriving at a simple point is harder. It requires taking complicated data, finding the gem of insight and then working and working the data down until your message is as simple and polished as you can get it.

The next step is conveying that message, where I am required to develop my presentation skills. Data analysts are quite typically quiet people who spend long periods interacting peacefully with rows and rows of data. It is therefore a fairly common challenge for data analysts to develop their 'people skills', and to find the confidence to stand up in front of people, present their data, persuade their audience to their way of thinking, and push for change in the business as a result of the findings. All of these steps are important, actually. It is little use for a business that analysts produce findings that don't stimulate any meaningful change. If this element is not present, they are merely collecting a pay check without providing any value. The insight must cause change for it to be useful. So, two elements are vital; the crafting of your message, and your ability to persuade.

And so it was with this realization that it occurred to me that

I'm actually not a scientist in the accepted sense. Whilst there is a science that I must know and use – such as statistics – there is another equally important element to what I do, which is the crafting of the scientific data; something one may characterize as an 'art'. Both the science and art of my job are vital, and if either is missing then I can't do my job effectively.

If I am unable to craft my message and persuade others, then my insight is not contributing to the business. Stakeholders either won't find my suggestions interesting, or they won't understand them, or they won't find them relevant. My influence in the business will therefore decline over time. Conversely, if I don't have the scientific knowledge and the skills to process the data and produce accurate results, then whilst I may be able to persuade my stakeholders to my way of thinking, I will be giving them incorrect information that will cause us to initiate actions that won't actually work. Again, my influence will decline as my advice won't produce results.

In many ways, I find that everything comes back to this required balance between knowledge and skills. Only if both are applied, whether you are a surgeon, a plumber, or a real-estate agent, can you be most effective. If everyone applied this posture of excellence to their work it would push us forward as a society, because both the heart (science) and the soul (art) of our work would be present to positively influence others.

The science and art of storytelling

by Sarah Perceval

I grew up in rural Surrey, with a childhood rich in craft and creativity. After training at drama school, I had a career as an actor in classical theatre. Discovering the Bahá'í Faith in my late 20s led me to think deeply about the material I was performing, and I reoriented my performance skills towards storytelling with interfaith and intercultural themes. I now live with my husband in the beautiful Ashdown Forest, discovering the joys of a part-time job which finances a full-time craft addiction.

The concept of the relationship between knowledge and skills, or science and art, reminds me of the method used to construct a story in order to perform it. The method begins by researching as many versions of that particular story as possible, then pursuing the version most authentic to the storyteller. One must think about the structure of the story, its place in history, particular cultural or religious delicacies to be aware of, themes one can bring out. Consideration is taken of the places where one must stick entirely to fact, the places one can embroider a little, the atmospheres one can evoke through word or gesture. After the knowledge is gathered, the skill of improvisation is used to rehearse it until it falls into a form which feels natural and comfortable to the storyteller.

A story has an internal skeleton – often referred to as 'the bare bones' – a basic structure that must be included in order to make the story stand up. It also has flesh; the flesh brings the story skeleton to life and helps it appeal to the particular audience to whom it is being told. It animates the skeleton and moves it, in some part, according to the interaction between the audience and the storyteller. One of the skills of a storyteller is to feel, in the moment, how the audience needs to be served through the telling of the story; in what mood is the audience? How much do they want to assist in the birthing of the story through interaction and participation? The storyteller becomes a kind of guide, taking the audience over the threshold of the story into the depths of their own imaginations and safely out the other side.

After the performance, a regular comment is 'How do you remember all those words?' Another of the skills of a storyteller is the persistence to be able to rehearse relentlessly, as the story never magically stands up without a good deal of hard work. Other skills to apply to the basic structural skeleton in order to bring it to life include delivery skills such as clear fluent expressive speech, awareness of eye contact, body language and gesture, the skill of exercising memory (something I am losing as I get older) and the skill of connecting to the 'inner spirit' of the story. A good storyteller becomes the story and disappears as the story is told. Storytelling is the garnering of research and accumulation of knowledge, then the use of theatre and communication skills to make that research come alive for an audience, to help the story stand up and live.

The understanding of the necessity of sciences and arts, knowledge and skills working together that I gained from the practice of storytelling now informs my forays into various crafts. I know the importance of first gathering knowledge – of how a new material behaves, which tools to use in what circumstance, consideration of scale, manipulation, construction and colour theory for instance –before, as in the practice of storytelling, the thing being made takes shape through the art of practice. The act of making brings tremendous fulfilment. It is a beautiful thing to fill a home with quilts, pottery, cushions, prints, plants and cake. Things made. Beauty is necessary for the soul, uplifts the spirit, and it's good to share the results of applying skills to knowledge through making a welcoming home. Using creativity for constructive acts bleads into all areas of my life and into my roles as a wife, daughter, stepmother, neighbour and friend.

I lean on the knowledge I have gathered through life and use the skill of creativity to manifest that knowledge in action. Another skill I often use is problem-solving, a skill I grew strong in due to dyslexia. At school I was reprimanded for the results of my dyslexia – terrible spelling, the need for extra thinking time, and the complete failure to learn my times tables. Now I use the heightened problem-solving skills dyslexia has gifted me with every single day.

These creative problem-solving skills and the knowledge I gained in sewing class gave me the confidence to volunteer at my local repair café when I first moved out of London and wanted to make friends in my new area. In working with the fabrics team, fellow volunteers have passed their knowledge on to me, particularly of darning. I now mentor a young woman from the village, and I so enjoy sitting together as we mend the items that are presented to us.

I find the concept of a repair café to be so positive. It

contributes, in its small, grassroots, village-centric way, to building a prosperous and positive world. The ethos of the café is physically constructive (as we mend the items brought in), socially constructive (as we sit with the person who brought the item in to show them how we are mending it), and environmentally constructive (as it stops a great many things ending up in landfill). It is sitting with your neighbours, mending small, broken pieces of life. It is service, togetherness, community, good will and positive action.

A small story to end with. At one session a man came in with a butterscotch-coloured hand-knitted blanket his granny had made him, which had a large hole in it. Over the course of our conversation it transpired that this man was recently divorced from his wife and was heartbroken. The blanket brought him the comfort of his well-loved grandmother. I found some fawn-coloured wool which would be a good match. 'Oh,' he said, 'actually, do you have any in bright red? I'd like a good honest visible mend, something that I can see has been repaired.' I hope that the visible mend he could see in his blanket helped him take a positive step forward into a new, reconstructed, chapter of his life.

The science and art of parenting

Janita McPharlin

My training and professional experience spans fine art, devised theatre, and the film industry in London. I have been fortunate enough to develop my creative capacities and apply them in various fields of expertise.

As women, of course, in addition to our careers, we are also nurturers, counsellors, guides, role models and educators, otherwise known as mothers. I have two boys whom I am privileged to be raising and the journey that I have embarked on has been a steep learning curve of understanding how to creatively apply the knowledge I have gained about spiritual education to the skill of parenting.

When we consider the purpose of God's revelation, we find that Bahá'u'lláh states that it is to 'effect a transformation in the whole character of mankind, a transformation that shall manifest itself both outwardly and inwardly, that shall affect both its inner life and external conditions'.[17]

This transformation has to begin within the family, as the family unit is the nucleus of human society. We are reminded by the Universal House of Justice that children 'bear the seeds of the character of future society'.[18]

The building blocks of character are the innate spiritual qualities that we spend a lifetime mining and polishing to enable us to be of service to humanity. If 'human happiness is founded upon spiritual behaviour'[19] then assisting our children to discover their inner treasures through a spiritual education is essential.

How is it that our parenting can provide a setting for the development of spiritual qualities and capacities latent in all human beings and in addition raise children who will assume responsibility for both the progress of society as well as their own spiritual growth?

For the last eight years I have been running a course called 'Spiritual Parenting' which has become a local form of social action by applying and diffusing knowledge in a neighbourhood setting.

It allows the participants to understand the purpose of educating our children spiritually and also to learn the skills to be able to guide and nurture them through childhood. This encourages an atmosphere of loving discipline, striving for excellence, the courage to accustom our children to hardship and a recognition of the importance of worship and service within the home environment. Children are deeply affected and influenced by their environment, especially by those in their community or immediate peer group. This calls for the need to educate all children rather than just our own.

This is where the dynamic pattern of action set out by the Ruhi Institute, which is fundamentally concerned with spiritual and moral empowerment, becomes the essential fabric of a neighbourhood. The skills that are developed through each book in the series of courses allow the participants to share the knowledge acquired from the educational content of the books. One of these patterns of action is the programme for the spiritual education of children.

The skill of teaching children is one that takes time to develop, but when approached creatively the results are hugely enhanced. The Universal House of Justice reminds us that the use of the arts is 'an important means of generating joy, strengthening bonds of unity, disseminating knowledge, and consolidating understanding'.[20] The different elements of a children's class allow for all of these outcomes to be present, but the skill of executing it with excellence is dependent on a teacher developing their capacity to prepare, practise and deliver the class with ease and enthusiasm.

It is when we see the multiplication of classes in neighbourhoods and the raising of more resources to be able to teach that we can begin to see the effect of this pattern of action on those who live in close proximity. The deepening of our knowledge of spiritual concepts that we can then impart to the children through the application of the skill of teaching is essential to building a prosperous world civilization, as it is the children who are the 'the most precious treasure a community can possess, for in them are the promise and guarantee of the future'.[21]

In order to achieve the vision, so urgently needed, of a united world we need to strengthen the ties that bind together the family unit and recognize that the habits and patterns of behaviour nurtured from a young age are carried into all aspects of future life. As 'Abdu'l-Bahá states, 'If love and agreement are manifest in a single family, that family will advance, become illumined and spiritual . . . This is likewise true of a city.'[22] He also reminds us that

> . . . if the sphere of unity be still further widened out, that is, if the inhabitants of a whole country develop peaceable hearts, and if with all their hearts and souls they yearn to cooperate with one another and to live in unity, and if they

> become kind and loving to one another, that country will achieve undying joy and lasting glory. Peace, will it have, and plenty, and vast wealth.[23]

We need to make great efforts to raise children who are promoters of the oneness of humanity and this is only achieved through nurturing a love for all people, an acute sense of justice and empathy for others. Only then will we fully understand what 'Abdu'l-Bahá means when he says:

> Compare the nations of the world to the members of a family. A family is a nation in miniature. Simply enlarge the circle of the household, and you have the nation. Enlarge the circle of nations, and you have all humanity. The conditions surrounding the family surround the nation. The happenings in the family are the happenings in the life of the nation. Would it add to the progress and advancement of a family if dissensions should arise among its members, all fighting, pillaging each other, jealous and revengeful of injury, seeking selfish advantage? Nay, this would be the cause of the effacement of progress and advancement. So it is in the great family of nations, for nations are but an aggregate of families.[24]

It is no small task to nurture and spiritually educate children against the backdrop of moral decay to which we are witness, but to persevere with the development of our own knowledge and skills is the most important as this allows us to translate Bahá'u'lláh's vision into reality.

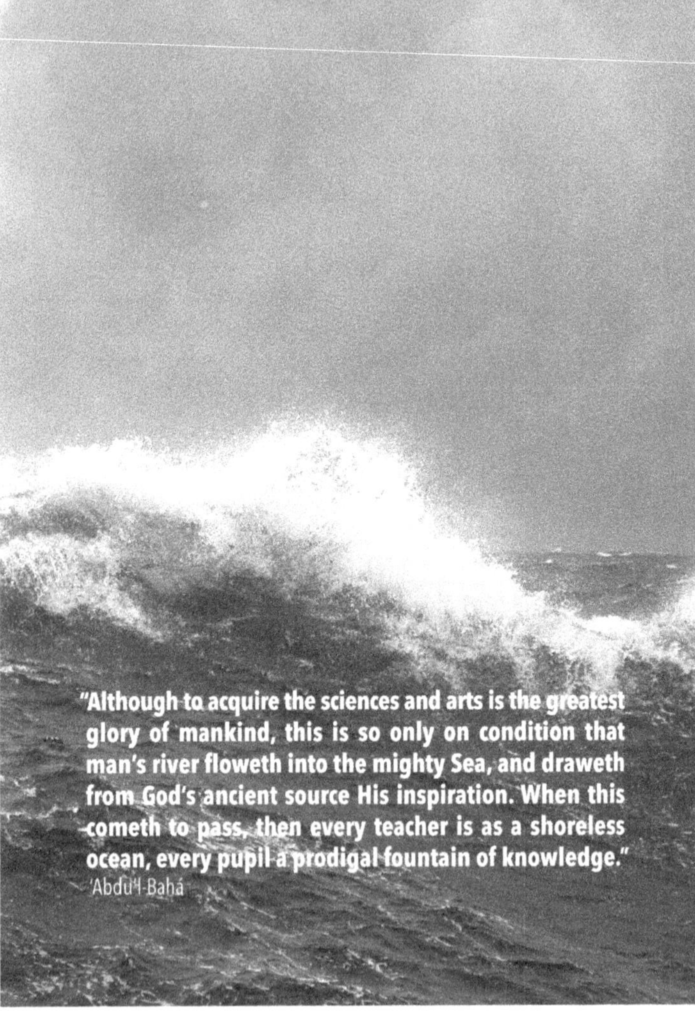
"Although to acquire the sciences and arts is the greatest glory of mankind, this is so only on condition that man's river floweth into the mighty Sea, and draweth from God's ancient source His inspiration. When this cometh to pass, then every teacher is as a shoreless ocean, every pupil a prodigal fountain of knowledge."
'Abdu'l-Bahá

7 My Sciences and Arts Applied

A lifetime of experience in education linked inextricably with the arts (in the conventional sense), plus years of organizing and planning large events, leads me to understand that my knowledge and my skills are in these areas especially, but I also recognize that I am striving to gain knowledge of my beliefs as a Bahá'í, and find ways to apply that knowledge in my everyday life.

I have a wealth of knowledge and skills around living life as a parent, a grandparent, a member of my local community, a human being striving to do my best. I now recognize that I am an intelligent creative human being who will never stop learning and applying that learning through whatever skills I want to acquire.

How have I applied my knowledge and skills over my lifetime?

*****

In the late 1980s I returned to the United Kingdom after 13 years living in Mauritius; however, my husband would take another 14 years to disentangle himself from his work in Mauritius, so I had to create my own life with the children. Amongst other things, I became involved in a local project with a good friend, Cecilia Smith. We decided that we would organize a Bahá'í summer school in the south of England. We had no previous experience, but we were confident we could do it. My father was an organizer, never happier than when challenged to make something happen. He was part of the small team who organized the first Bahá'í World Congress in London in 1963, so I had a great example to follow! We set about finding a venue, and with a group of friends planned the event. This was the first of several schools that we organized until the task was taken over by others.

The first venue was a local school. It was not a boarding school, so had no sleeping facilities, but we were undaunted. Classrooms were made into dormitories, and the catering was done by everyone helping in teams each day, with a couple of people planning and organizing the meals. Courses were offered, although looking back I have no recollection of what they were, and I have no records from that time to remind me.

It was great fun, and a real bonding experience with everyone playing their part to make it happen. This was the first of several Bahá'í summer schools that we helped organize, and was where Cecilia and I gained the confidence, experience, knowledge and skills for our next adventure.

The Bahá'í Academy for the Arts, 1993–2010

Beginnings

It began with very local activities in the late 1980s, initiated by Cecilia, who offered her large back garden for young people, both Bahá'ís and their friends, to come and camp and spend time learning and socializing together.

This group was particularly interested in dance and drama, and formed themselves into a performing group called Youth Quake. Both my children were involved in this early stage, although my daughter Janita was more inclined to performance than my son Jamil.

Youth Quake toured the country, with supportive parents, right up to the Shetland Islands. They presented dance performances in the towns along the way, and spawned other similar groups of energetic youngsters across the United Kingdom.

Second Bahá'í World Congress, 1992

The Youth Quake group was then given the opportunity to perform at the Youth Congress as part of the second Bahá'í World Congress, held in New York in 1992. They performed with great energy and enthusiasm as part of a unique historical event.

For Cecilia and myself, attending the Congress, it was the use of creative ways of utilizing music, drama and storytelling as the backbone of the Congress to transmit knowledge, understanding, feelings and emotions, rather than as 'entertainment', that inspired us to consider what we might do in the United Kingdom. What could we do to encourage young people in the UK to develop their skills in the 'arts', as we understood it at that time. As we had spent the previous few years together organizing summer schools, we had acquired the necessary understanding and skills from that perspective, so we were confident and excited by the challenge. However, we had no idea that it was to take over our lives for the next seventeen years.

First Academy event

In 1993 the Bahá'í Academy for the Arts was born. It was a very small one-week residential event in that first year, which we titled The Performing Arts Summer Academy with an attendance of twenty-five, mostly young people, all local to the UK, and including two organizers. There were three courses offered that year – dance, singing and drama. It grew over the seventeen years of its existence to welcome nearly three hundred participants who, between the ages of three and 93, arrived from all over the world, with a large selection of courses offered each year generating a buzz of creativity and an enthusiasm for achievement.

Concepts behind the Academy model

Over time we began to recognize that there were specific concepts underpinning the Academy. We started out with the goal of offering the participants the opportunity to develop their creative skills in an environment inspired by the Bahá'í teachings, but as time passed, we became aware that an educational model was evolving, simply because we recognized what enabled participants to fulfil their potential.

- Love was the foundation of the event . . . love of creativity, love of learning and the educational process, and a deep love for the teachings of the Bahá'í Faith.

- There was a sincere belief that every single human being has gems hidden within them; they need encouragement in the right environment for these gems to emerge and shine.

- The environment needed to be encouraging, nurturing, empowering – but also challenging to enable participants to reach their full potential.

- Personal excellence as a goal was also key; no competition, just aiming to do the best possible in the time available.

- An environment of respect where there was no criticism, no judgement and no comparison created a safe learning space for all.

- Discipline, both in behaviour and attitude, of all involved in the event was also hugely important.

These concepts became recognized as the hallmark of the Academy and enabled many participants to emerge with new knowledge and skills plus confidence and a renewed belief in their creative capacity and spiritual strength.

Three facets

As the event evolved, three facets emerged: the spiritual, the educational and the arts. In 2000 we designed a logo (below) that sought to express the relationship between the three facets, and their relationship to the ocean of the writings of the Bahá'í Faith as the source of inspiration and guidance.

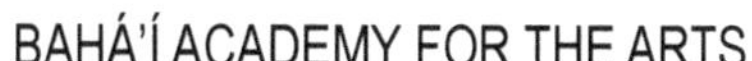

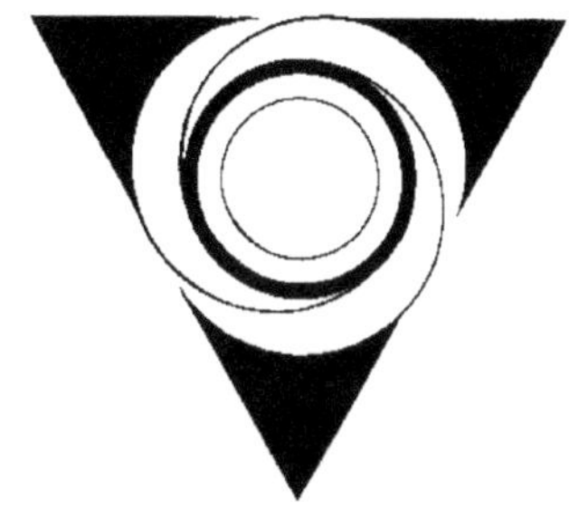

At this time, we perceived the arts in the traditional way: performance, visual and written arts. The event provided inspirational educational opportunities with tutors from around the world, but it was the spiritual roots that gave it life and purpose and energy. A learning model evolved that proved highly successful and was life-changing for many participants in numerous ways.

However, evidence in the archives shows that early on I and others began to question why we separated the arts from the sciences. The references to science and art in the Bahá'í writings suggested a totally integrated relationship, and we had conversations around broadening out the programme: could it become the Bahá'í Academy for the Arts and Sciences? Yet at that time this would have been, in reality, translated into separate 'subjects', as we did not understand the real connections between them.

Belief in capacity and the principle of excellence

I realized very soon that all the learning principles and practice that I utilized within my professional life (teaching adults to draw), that in turn were based on my spiritual beliefs, were expressed in this event. It was imbued with love and enthusiasm, but the foundation was the total belief that everyone had the capacity to achieve – not accomplishment seen against an arbitrary outside standard, but an achievement of a personal excellence. The principle of pushing a learner to the edge of their learning in an environment that simultaneously encourages and challenges them, and also totally believes that they can achieve, is very powerful. It carries those who are less confident until they can believe in themselves and take over their own progress, but it also allows participants at all levels of achievement to work together equally because each one is on their individual journey. So it is not about the starting point, it is about what can be achieved in the time available.

Organization

The principle of excellence was carried through to the organization of the event where the team, around six in number, endeavoured to offer the best within their capacity, paying attention to every detail of the planning and delivery of the event as well as the overall structure of love and support for both the participants and those working as tutors and the numerous support staff.

The coordination of the Academy was almost a full-time occupation; as soon as one event finished, the process of evaluation and reflection and planning for the following year began immediately. Eventually we would make a plan for three years, so we knew we would have a rolling programme of courses that was constantly changing over time, that allowed each tutor, if they wished, to develop their knowledge and skills over a period of time, as they gained experience.

Over the years, many highly knowledgeable and skilled

people offered their support, tutoring courses, planning, organizing, assisting on site, and so the model developed and became known internationally.

Learning to handle challenges

The development was gradual, so as experience was gained and a process of very regular reflection on learning encouraged the event to evolve and grow, and as we, as organizers, grew in maturity and understanding, the Academy began to cater for larger numbers. Inevitably, we learned how to deal with some challenging and traumatic events.

Perhaps one traumatic event that has stayed in my mind was when the Ram family, who regularly attended the event, chose in July 2001 to gather the whole family from around the world to come together at the Academy, that year being held in Sidcot School in Somerset.

Dariush and Mihan Ram, their son and daughter Vafa and Guita, and the grandchildren Adora, Mateen and Tala were all present. On the first night of the Academy Dariush very unexpectedly passed away during the night. In total unity we surrounded the members of the family and arrangements were made for the funeral service to be part of the Academy programme, enabling the family of Dariush to mourn together within a loving atmosphere amongst friends; the funeral took place on the final day.

Twenty years later, in 2021, Guita wrote about the tragic circumstances:

> It was indeed a shocking and sad experience for our family because we had come to the Arts Academy looking forward to having an uplifting and positive time, especially after our three-day visit to the Holy Land. And although quite unexpectedly our father passed away on the night of our arrival, losing him while amongst a hundred friends and well-wishers meant we could bear the unbearable with calm and confident hearts. Looking back on it, it was

particularly a relief that our children were surrounded with many friends young and old to share their grief and come to terms with this sadness. Our father had told us that during our three-day visit, he begged Bahá'u'lláh to allow him to teach again as his poor sight and hearing was hindering him from teaching. When leaving Haifa, he was very happy, as he felt Bahá'u'lláh would soon grant his wish.

Dariush Ram was a lover of and a promoter of arts. He was an avid photographer, an acclaimed painter and a celebrated violinist in his youth among his Bahá'í friends and family. As such, it was quite a place for him to part with his earthly life while amongst many other artists. Being a lawyer by training, it was easy and important for Dariush to lead a coherent life, in exerting both the right and left side of the brain. When searching for solutions, he balanced artistic senses with rational and scientific approaches to reach the conclusion through logical thinking.

He passed away on the first night and was buried on the last day. My son Shafa was at a Junior Youth camp at Landegg at the time, but along with my husband Shohab, joined us at the end of the week. Our aunt and uncles from California and New Zealand and our cousin from Ottawa also joined us in time for the burial. While my mother and I went back to London on the next day to prepare for the funeral, and Vafa intended to leave too so as to not impact the Academy's normal proceedings, the warm suggestions of some friends impelled us to hold the funeral on the last day of the Academy. For example, May Hofman suggested that this would give a good opportunity to the Bahá'í community to celebrate happy times but also learn how to share the sad moments of our lives. Similarly, the Academy's organizers embraced this situation with such love and warmth, and lent us their assistance which made it possible for the funeral programme to be held at the Academy in the presence of all participants, as if they all sent him off on his eternal journey. This made those six days memorable not only for the family, but also for many of the participants, even after 20 years.

Age range

From the outset the Academy offered week-long courses in the arts, at first from the age of 11 upwards, and then as we gained confidence and learned how to manage a broader age range it eventually catered for all ages from three years upwards. The three-year-olds were with a parent or carer in a course that focused on creative play, assisting the parents/carers to gain more confidence in their abilities to play creatively . . . children do it naturally! All the younger age groups were catered for with courses that were designed specifically for them, while those who were 15 or over were considered adults, our oldest participant being in her nineties. In contrast to the world in general where youth and adults are seen as incompatible and are often separated, we made the decision to integrate the 'youth' with the 'adults', because we wanted them to contribute to each other's learning, In the beginning this decision created anxiety for both students and tutors, but soon simply became part of how the Academy worked.

High expectations

The Bahá'í Academy for the Arts became known for its high expectations of all attendees, in terms of behaviour and attitudes. We had a Code of Conduct that was applicable to all those present, whether they were tutors, organizers, students or helpers. It was created around spiritual principles and was worded in such a way as to be positive rather than negative; it was not a list of 'do nots' but rather what to strive for:

- To aim for **personal excellence**
- To be ***constantly sensitive*** to the differing needs of each other and encourage **mutual and self-respect**
- To adhere to high **spiritual and moral principles** at all times

- To **practise moderation** in all things pertaining to language, dress and behaviour

- To ensure **punctual attendance** at all sessions, ready to **give and receive the maximum**

- To resolve any issues or concerns **through consultation**

We managed behaviour with the Code of Conduct as the core values, and a huge amount of love and many hours of consultation! The behaviour was always separated from the person, so the consultations were around how behaviour could be changed. We learned very quickly that the younger ones, although they would kick against the 'rules', were the first to register the following year, so we felt we were on the right track.

We provided the opportunity also for small groups or individuals who needed space to develop their creative practice or ideas, so we had musicians, dancers and writers with varying practical needs working alongside the provision of courses. Some individuals just needed a creative space to work on a project, or groups of practitioners needed a specialist space for their art, but all were happy to be in a highly charged creative atmosphere with everything provided!

Sharing learning

We encouraged every course to share their learning at the end of the week. In the beginning much time and focus was on the 'final presentations', but it was realized, over time, that the process of learning and creating was far more important than the end product, so we quickly changed the emphasis to sharing 'work in progress'. Each course was offered a space to share, be that by exhibition, performance or other means.

The power of spiritual concepts

The outcomes of this event were fascinating, with many stories of lives being changed, or turned around because of the opportunities to work with highly skilled tutors in an environment of total belief in capacity, and the encouragement to achieve personal excellence. The strong spiritual foundation that permeated everything we did and guided our decision making was a major factor, it offered a far deeper experience than an 'arts summer school'.

What this experience demonstrated was the power of spiritual concepts to inform, inspire and guide practical actions, that in turn, had themselves the power to transform, encourage and motivate achievement. Here are stories from three participants who describe their personal experiences of the Academy.

Martin Kerr, who attended the Academy first as a child, says:

> I have very happy memories of attending the Arts Academy, and the experience shaped me as an artist and a Bahá'í, giving me confidence, skills, inspiration, role models and a sense of community that have carried me forward for the rest of my life. I'm always grateful for your love, dedication, skill and care in creating those experiences for all of us.

Martin has become a well-respected singer /songwriter in Canada since the Academy years.

Jessica Naish shared these memories of her experiences:

> The Arts Academy formed so much of my creative and Bahá'í identity. It was the space where as a friend of the Faith initially, I could explore the spiritual principles within the Writings in a space that was so free of judgement, it was loving and brimming with a desire for creative and spiritual excellence. It was a place where one knew friendships would be formed, new skills would be developed, and learning was at its heart. The love of God could be expressed and shared so generously that on leaving, one's soul would be

> overflowing and it was impossible not to be transformed.
>
> I remember the devotionals always being so beautiful, it attracted me as a seeker and as a new Baha'i. I loved how every art form found expression through myriad people and moments and each was tethered delicately yet boldly to humble service to humanity. The team's dedication to careful planning and preparation, reflection and adjustments, as the Academy developed, was an inspiration for me as a practitioner. So distinctive and often contrasting to the way other occasions in wider society are organized.

Finally, Alyssa shares her story:

> I first went to the Arts Academy when I was 8 years old. I grew up in a town of only two Bahá'í families so getting to spend a week with other Bahá'ís my age was a glorious experience. We did a production of *The Lion King* in a week and I had lots of fun!
>
> The following year the AA team decided to change the age range, you had to be 10 to attend the event. I sadly was only 9, however, an exception was made for me and 9-year-old Claire who was also allowed to attend again! I felt so special! It made me feel loved and safe. We performed *Evita*, I believe this was the year that Natasha had to deal with me crying a lot! This was also the year I first set the fire alarm off and the fire brigade came to the school. I am eternally sorry for that!
>
> I also attended the Arts Academy for the next two years. I remember loving every minute! It was so great as a young person to get to know Bahá'ís from all over the world and to get to hang out with others my own age, and many other ages. One of the great things about the Academy and its atmosphere, was that age didn't seem to matter, everyone was open and friendly and happy to chat to each other. As a child, the Arts Academy was a safe place to feel loved, when that wasn't always true in the rest of my life.
>
> The next time I attended the Academy was when I was

15, I was on an adult course. I know around that age I did a mask workshop week with Jess, and a singing course with Richard, and another singing course with Fleur. In my teenage years, the Arts Academy really helped me find my path in life.

In these years I met so many people who have had an immense influence on my life. When I was 17 Richard and Lou came to the Arts Academy with 8-week-old Joia. I had asked if I could hold her and then I lost track of where her parents were. I seem to remember that there was a lot of time where I was holding an 8-week-old baby without a clue where her parents were, and with other people assuming she was my baby, and none of that was a problem because we were at the Arts Academy and everything has to be OK when you are there. This forged a lifelong friendship; I visited them every school holiday that I could and that led to me living in Wellingborough, after I finished my A-Levels, until I figured out what I wanted to be when I grew up!

Again, there is a gap until the final two years of the Arts Academy 2009/2010. In 2009 I was camping and I had borrowed Richard and Lou's eight-man tunnel tent. I had arrived in plenty of time to set up my tent and be available to help others with setting up theirs as they arrived. I had just finished setting up my GIANT tent and two ladies pulled up to start pitching their tent, I remember it being tiny, in my mind it was like a small child's garden pop-up tent. They were discussing how they wouldn't both fit into the tent and maybe one of them could sleep in the car, and one of them in the tent, swapping each night. But this was the Arts Academy, where generosity and friendship abound! So having an eight-man tent to myself seemed ludicrous and selfish! I offered these two ladies a two-man compartment each in the other wing of the tent from my four-man section. Each of these compartments was larger than their tent in which both of them had planned to sleep.

This was also the year that I discovered my career path! One of the evening sessions was a play by Sarah Munro,

> and I had been asked to help her by stage-managing the performance. The following year, I had made it on to the team! I was technical support for the Arts Academy! To be able to be of service to an institution that had shaped me as a person was a real honour and delight. The Arts Academy was a place of safety and love, it was a week where unity in diversity happened in practice, and acceptance and joy were an essential part of the experience. For me my best guess is that I attended nine Arts Academies and to think that in only nine actual weeks of being at the Arts Academy it changed my life is astonishing!

Alyssa is now a full-time stage manager. Her account also demonstrates the power of the arts to transform and inspire; it is only as time has gone by that it is realized how many of the young people who attended the Academy courses went on to make their careers in various creative roles, as described in the stories above.

Questioning accepted understandings

Looking back now, in 2023, thirteen years after the Arts Academy closed, I also understand that we were trapped in an old-world view of the arts. We ignored the relationship with science, because arts and sciences were perceived as being separate, unrelated, mutually exclusive. However, I also know that this was because we had been educated to think that this was correct by a system rooted in a history of cultural events, and that these concepts had never been questioned.

However, it was during the development of the Academy that I and others began to question why there was such a gulf between what we read in the Bahá'í Writings about art and science and what was experienced in the world at large. It was at this time also that I read Ken Robinson's book *Out of Our Minds*. This book excited and inspired me, and encouraged me to question accepted understanding, especially as it resonated with my own beliefs both as a Bahá'í and as an educator.

Those early questions led to my research to find answers, and to bring an alternative understanding of the relationship between science and art to the attention of those interested. However, I realize now that this relationship is simply part of our lives as human beings, there is nothing in life that does not utilize our knowledge and skills or our sciences and arts.

A moment of encouragement

I spent many years doubting if what I was thinking made any sense, as I could not find others exploring these concepts. It was only in 2017 that by pure chance I watched Mr Hooper Dunbar give a presentation for the Association for Bahá'í Studies Conference in the United States, in which he interrupted his presentation to share something on art. His 'sharing' lasted all of a minute or so, but he drew on his understanding of the writings on science and art to say that art is the application of science. I was totally blown away and asked him for confirmation of these concepts, which he supplied. As yet, the compilation on science and art to which he refers is not yet available but will, I presume, be published in due course when the time is right.

This chance encounter, which echoed what I had come to understand myself, allowed me to feel confident to share the ideas with others. The response was positive, leading to creating Zoom presentations during COVID lockdown in 2020/21, and then finally bringing the concepts together into a book.

In the summer of 2023, the Academy team came together to organize a weekend event that was to celebrate 30 years since it was founded. The event set out to consider the impact of the Academy on its participants, and how, since that time, they have applied that learning in communities and neighbourhoods. It was a very focused weekend of intense conversations, immersion in creative processes, study of the guidance and presentations that shared learning and understanding – all this in the context of the present Nine-Year Plan and the guidance of the Universal House of Justice to explore how to draw more effectively on the power of the arts to transform society, to generate joy, disseminate knowledge and consolidate understanding. It is too early to know the impact of this event, but for those who attended it seems to have been a powerful experience in many ways, and there are plans to hold further events that focus on this theme.

Drawing on the right side of the brain, 1994–2014

Looking back on my own teaching experience of around 45 years, mainly with adults teaching drawing, my greatest insight has been around understanding the process of how people learn.

I spent 13 years in Mauritius training art teachers for secondary schools, and when I returned to the United Kingdom, I discovered a book by Betty Edwards called *Drawing on the Right Side of the Brain*. This book, and the unique approach it suggested, set me on a journey of designing and delivering a course for adults that changed my own approach to drawing and enabled many others to gain confidence and skills they thought they didn't have.

I worked originally within local adult education until the British Government introduced the focus on gaining qualifications; my students were simply not interested in that, and I began working independently, and took my students with me. I had designed and developed a three-year course called *'So You Think You Can't Draw . . .but really you can!'* and I offered this and evolved the course over around twenty years.

I know I was influenced by my Bahá'í beliefs, which encouraged personal excellence, and taught me that every individual has capacity, and thus, if they want to, can learn to draw. I gradually developed a teaching approach that focused on the individual's learning journey, stressing their uniqueness, so they focused on their own pathway and never compared themselves to anyone else. This encouraged a mutually supportive environment because no one felt they were competing with anyone else, only with themselves. This process was built on constant encouragement but also constant challenge; as soon as one skill was achieved then another challenge was presented, so pushing them always to the edge of their individual learning.

Public exhibitions

This teaching approach was linked to a method of learning to draw that focused not on learning 'how to draw', but on learning 'how to *see* for drawing'. The outcomes of learning to see in a specific way for drawing, combined with the teaching methodology, were dramatically successful. At the end of the three-year course the students would tell the story of their journey from very first pre-instruction drawings to final pieces in a public exhibition. Visitors to the exhibition were fascinated and wanted to have the same experience themselves, so the course became self-propagating, and was in constant demand.

Bahá'í summer schools, 2013–2020

The Academy events and my professional life ran alongside the annual Bahá'í Summer Schools. I had grown up attending summer schools from the age of nine or so, and can remember the early experience of two-week summer schools spent in the company of many amazing people who were the early founders of the Bahá'í community in the United Kingdom. Who would have believed then that I would be involved in organizing summer schools myself in later years.

The vision, the science, the art – in practice

After the Bahá'í Academy for the Arts closed in 2010 I had various roles in supporting the organization of summer schools. In 2013 I was given the responsibility to support the individuals who were tutoring courses at the summer school. I created a guide for the tutors; when I read it now, it demonstrates how I was beginning to apply my understanding of the interrelationship between science and art. I am not sure anyone else really understood the concepts I was presenting, but they made huge sense to me!

During this period of assisting with summer schools, either organizing or tutoring courses, I felt conflicted over how the arts were being utilized, but it would take several years to arrive at a point where I had the confidence to share my research, which appears to demonstrate that when these narrow interpretations and understandings are broadened and science is understood to be about the 'accumulation of knowledge' and art is the 'skilled application of that knowledge', either in the sense of an object or an experience, then the opportunities to include everyone in the process of generating and applying knowledge seems logical.

Knowledge and skills are inseparable

The knowledge and its application are inseparable. So, in the context of a summer school, whether the subject or theme be the spiritual education of children, the Bahá'í administration or a spiritual approach to economic problems or climate change or the study of early Bahá'í history, the amassing of knowledge about each one is a prerequisite to finding the best way to deliver that knowledge and to offer the participants a learning opportunity through a variety of teaching strategies, and through this experience they themselves perfect their own gems, gain skills and learn how to share with others.

I now understand the integral relationship between the knowledge and the application of the knowledge using learnt skills, or in the language of Bahá'u'lláh about the education of children: 'to master every kind of learning, and make them eager to become skilled in every art'.

Return to university

I went back to university later in life, once my children had left the nest, and I was waiting for my husband to return to the United Kingdom. I wanted to explore why adults draw like children and how a specific method of teaching children and adults, 'how to see for drawing', rather than learning how to draw, linked to a very focused teaching methodology, can create confidence and develop skills. My main interest has always been how to devise a learning methodology that was inclusive and encouraging, yet challenging, and nurtured everyone to achieve their potential.

Teaching children's classes 2016–2023

Assisting teaching Grades 1 -5

This has been a truly life-confirming experience from several perspectives. I have been a part of the spiritual education of my own grandchildren alongside many other children, and been able to experience the Ruhi Institute concepts in practice.

My daughter was keen to provide a spiritual education for her own children and others from the time they were very small, so she offered toddler classes that included other children besides her own. Her two boys, consequently, alongside other children, are progressing through the complete series of grades; both the boys, having completed Grade 5, are now part of a Junior Youth group. My own teaching experience has, I hope, supported her in her journey of discovering how to plan, organize and teach classes over the years.

To watch these young people grow and develop in understanding, and acquire the language to explain what they are learning, is magical. It confirms the important and unique role of the Ruhi Institute process in providing a firm foundation for children in acquiring spiritual knowledge and perfecting skills which they can then apply in their own everyday lives.

My role has been as support teacher, taking responsibility for sections of the lessons such as storytelling and the creative activities. We have had so much joy over the years working with groups of children, and of course have devoted many hours to preparation and planning – all worthwhile when the outcomes are seen in the children.

Final words

As the Universal House of Justice wrote in its Riḍván message of 2010:

> . . . there are certain fundamental concepts that all should bear in mind. One is the centrality of knowledge to social existence. The perpetuation of ignorance is a most grievous form of oppression; it reinforces the many walls of prejudice that stand as barriers to the realization of the oneness of humankind, at once the goal and operating principle of Bahá'u'lláh's Revelation. Access to knowledge is the right of every human being, and participation in its generation, application and diffusion a responsibility that all must shoulder in the great enterprise of building a prosperous world civilization – each individual according to his or her talents and abilities. Justice demands universal participation.

I hope that, through asking questions and searching for answers, I have been able to demonstrate that our present understanding of the relationship between science and art is based on misinterpretations and misconceptions that have been reinforced over the years through our western education system.

When these narrow interpretations and understandings are broadened and science is understood to be the 'accumulation of knowledge' and art the 'skilled application of that knowledge', expressed either as an object or an experience, then the opportunities to include everyone in the process of generating and applying and diffusing knowledge seems logical.

Thought of in this way, art *is* the application of science, but only if the understanding of both science and art is broad and inclusive, where science is seen as any system of knowledge and art any form of practice that enables that system of knowledge to be applied in practice.

However, an understanding that has come about through many generations of educational experience, particularly in the west, will take time to adjust to new thinking, and I accept that situation with humility, but I have confidence that as the Bahá'í writings become more influential and understood at a deeper level, then the inseparable relationship between science and art will become an accepted concept. This will enable all human beings, to recognize the gems they have hidden within the mines of their inmost selves and enable them to bring those gems to the surface, and cut and polish them and finally to offer them in service to mankind, with the one aim of creating a prosperous world civilization that honours every aspect of our planet, including every human being.

Let me finish with the Riḍván message of 2023 from the Universal House of Justice:

> In this new series of Plans, increasing attention needs to be given to other processes that seek to enhance the life of a community – for example, by improving public health, protecting the environment, or drawing more effectively on the power of the arts. What is required for all these complementary aspects of a community's well-being to advance is, of course, the capacity to engage in systematic learning in all these areas – a capacity that draws on insights arising from the Teachings and the accumulated store of human knowledge generated through scientific enquiry. As this capacity grows, much will be accomplished over the coming decades.

Appendix
Arts, Science and Education
A Compilation of Bahá'í Writings

A personal collection by the author

I brought together this compilation while I was researching for the book, and found that I could not separate education, science and art as they were far too intertwined. I also recognize that this compilation is far from complete.

I made the decision, therefore, to include all quotations that I discovered, organised by author rather than theme. I hope that it will be a voyage of discovery and inspiration to readers.

From the writings of the Báb

1. No created thing shall ever attain its paradise unless it appeareth in its highest prescribed degree of perfection. For instance, this crystal representeth the paradise of the stone whereof its substance is composed. Likewise, there are various stages in the paradise for the crystal itself . . . So long as it was stone it was worthless, but if it attaineth the excellence of ruby – a potentiality which is latent in it – how much a carat will it be worth? Consider likewise every created thing.[1]

2. Whoever possesseth power over anything must elevate it to its uttermost perfection that it not be deprived of its own paradise. For example, the paradise of a sheet of paper on which a few excellent lines are inscribed is that it be refined with patterns of gold illumination, adornment, and excellence that are customary for the most exalted parchment scrolls. Then the possessor of that paper hath elevated it to its utmost degree of

glory. Should he know of a higher degree of refinement and fail to manifest it upon that paper, he would deprive it of its paradise, and he would be held accountable, for why hast thou, despite the possession of the means, withheld the effusion of grace and favour?[2]

3. It is forbidden to people to cause anything that is defective to appear if they have the power to perfect that thing. For example if someone were to build a house and not bring it to whatever perfection it is capable of achieving, then there will not be an instant that the angels will not be calling out to God for his punishment, even the atoms of that building will also do this. For every thing within its own limits desires to attain to the highest point of its limits. And if a person has the ability to do this for it but does not, then he will be held responsible by it.[3]

4. It is not permitted to anyone to write a single letter of the Bayán except in the most beautiful of handwritings. 'Most beautiful' here means the best that each individual is capable of; not beyond that, but not less than that either. This is so that the spirit that is attached to every letter of the Bayan may be raised to the highest level that is possible in this contingent world within its limitations such that no thing may be seen among the believers in the Bayan except that that thing be in the highest state of perfection possible for it.

However, all this is on the condition that one keeps within one's capacity, not that one should put oneself in hardship on account of anything. For God desires not to look upon a believer in grief or distress. No! Rather everyone should carry out these obligations according to their ability.[4]

5. Say! We verily have perfected Our handiwork in the creation of the heavens, earth, whatever lieth between them, and in all things; will ye not then behold?. . . Perfect ye then your own handiwork in all that ye produce with your hands working through the handiwork of God. Then would this indeed be a handiwork of God, the Help in Peril, the SelfSubsisting. Waste

ye not that which God createth with your hands through your handiwork; rather, make manifest in them the perfection of industry or craft, be it a large and mass product or a small and retail one. For verily one who perfecteth his handiwork indeed attaineth certitude in the perfection of the handiwork of God within his own being.[5]

From the writings of Bahá'u'lláh

1. The Purpose of the one true God, exalted be His glory, in revealing Himself unto men is to lay bare those gems that lie hidden within the mine of their true and inmost selves.[6]

2. Regard man as a mine rich in gems of inestimable value. Education can, alone, cause it to reveal its treasures, and enable mankind to benefit therefrom.[7]

3. At the outset of every endeavour, it is incumbent to look to the end of it. Of all the arts and sciences, set the children to studying those which will result in advantage to man, will ensure his progress and elevate his rank. Thus the noisome odours of lawlessness will be dispelled, and thus through the high endeavours of the nation's leaders, all will live cradled, secure and in peace.

The Great Being saith: The learned of the day must direct the people to acquire those branches of knowledge which are of use, that both the learned themselves and the generality of mankind may derive benefits therefrom.[8]

4. Knowledge is one of the wondrous gifts of God. It is incumbent upon everyone to acquire it. Such arts and material means as are now manifest have been achieved by virtue of His knowledge and wisdom which have been revealed in Epistles and Tablets through His Most Exalted Pen – a Pen out of whose treasury pearls of wisdom and utterance and the arts and crafts of the world are brought to light.[9]

5. In the third Tajalli (effulgence) of the Book of Tajalliyat (Book of Effulgences) We have mentioned:

'Arts, crafts and sciences uplift the world of being, and are conducive to its exaltation. Knowledge is as wings to man's life, and a ladder for his ascent. Its acquisition is incumbent upon everyone. The knowledge of such sciences, however, should be acquired as can profit the peoples of the earth, and not those that begin with words and end with words. Great indeed is the claim of scientists and craftsmen on the peoples of the world . . .

In truth, knowledge is a veritable treasure for man, and a source of glory, of bounty, of joy, of exaltation, of cheer and gladness unto him. Happy the man that cleaveth unto it, and woe betide the heedless.[10]

6. It is incumbent upon the children to exert themselves to the utmost in acquiring the art of reading and writing . . . Writing skills that will provide for urgent needs will be enough for some; and then it is better and more fitting that they should spend their time in studying those branches of knowledge which are of use.

As for what the Supreme Pen hath previously set down, the reason is that in every art and skill, God loveth the highest perfection.[11]

7. The soul that hath remained faithful to the Cause of God, and stood unwaveringly firm in His Path shall, after his ascension, be possessed of such power that all the worlds which the Almighty hath created can benefit through him. Such a soul provideth, at the bidding of the Ideal King and Divine Educator, the pure leaven that leaveneth the world of being, and furnisheth the power through which the arts and wonders of the world are made manifest.[12]

8. The Sun of Truth is the Word of God upon which dependeth the education of those who are endowed with the power of understanding and of utterance. It is the true spirit and the heavenly water, through whose aid and gracious providence all

things have been and will be quickened. Its appearance in every mirror is conditioned by the colour of that mirror. For instance, when its light is cast upon the mirrors of the hearts of the wise, it bringeth forth wisdom. In like manner when it manifesteth itself in the mirrors of the hearts of craftsmen, it unfoldeth new and unique arts, and when reflected in the hearts of those that apprehend the truth it revealeth wondrous tokens of true knowledge and discloseth the verities of God's utterance.[13]

9. O people of Bahá! The source of crafts, sciences and arts is the power of reflection. Make ye every effort that out of this ideal mine there may gleam forth such pearls of wisdom and utterance as will promote the well-being and harmony of all the kindreds of the earth.[14]

10. Unveiled and unconcealed, this Wronged One hath, at all times, proclaimed before the face of all the peoples of the world that which will serve as the key for unlocking the doors of sciences, of arts, of knowledge, of well-being, of prosperity and wealth.[15]

11. Teach ye your children so that they may peruse the divine verses every morn and eve. God hath prescribed unto every father to educate his children, both boys and girls, in the sciences and in morals, and in crafts and professions.[16]

12. O Inmost Heart of this Temple! We have made thee the dawning-place of Our knowledge and the dayspring of Our wisdom unto all who are in heaven and on earth. From thee have We caused all sciences to appear, and unto thee shall We cause them to return. And from thee shall We bring them forth a second time. Such, indeed, is Our promise, and potent are We to effect Our purpose. Erelong shall We bring into being through thee exponents of new and wondrous sciences, of potent and effective crafts, and shall make manifest through them that which the heart of none of Our servants hath yet conceived. Thus do We bestow upon whom We will whatsoever We desire, and thus do We withdraw from whom

We will what We had once bestowed. Even so do We ordain whatsoever We please through Our behest.[17]

13. This Day, O Shaykh, hath never been, nor is it now, the Day whereon man-made arts and sciences can be regarded as a true standard for men, since it hath been recognized that He Who was wholly unversed in any of them hath ascended the throne of purest gold, and occupied the seat of honor in the council of knowledge, whilst the acknowledged exponent and repository of these arts and sciences remained utterly deprived. By 'arts and sciences' is meant those which begin with words and end with words. Such arts and sciences, however, as are productive of good results, and bring forth their fruit, and are conducive to the well-being and tranquility of men have been, and will remain, acceptable before God. Wert thou to give ear to My voice, thou wouldst cast away all thy possessions, and wouldst set thy face towards the Spot wherein the ocean of wisdom and of utterance hath surged, and the sweet savors of the loving-kindness of thy Lord, the Compassionate, have wafted.[18]

14. One of the names of God is the Fashioner. He loveth craftsmanship. Therefore any of His servants who manifesteth this attribute is acceptable in the sight of this Wronged One. Craftsmanship is a book among the books of divine sciences, and a treasure among the treasures of His heavenly wisdom. This is a knowledge with meaning, for some of the sciences are brought forth by words and come to an end with words.[19]

15. 'We have permitted you to read such sciences as are profitable unto you, not such as end in idle disputation' (para. 77). The Bahá'í writings enjoin the acquisition of knowledge and the study of the arts and sciences. Bahá'ís are admonished to respect people of learning and accomplishment, and are warned against the pursuit of studies that are productive only of futile wrangling. In His Tablets Bahá'u'lláh counsels the believers to study such sciences and arts as are *'useful'* and would further *'the progress and advancement'* of society, and He cautions against

sciences which *'begin with words and end with words'*, the pursuit of which leads to *'idle disputation'*. Shoghi Effendi, in a letter written on his behalf, likened sciences that begin with words and end with words to 'fruitless excursions into metaphysical hair-splittings', and, in another letter, he explained that what Bahá'u'lláh primarily intended by such 'sciences' are 'those theological treatises and commentaries that encumber the human mind rather than help it to attain the truth'.[20]

16. Strain every nerve to acquire both inner and outer perfections, for the fruit of the human tree hath ever been and will ever be perfections both within and without. It is not desirable that a man be left without knowledge or skills, for he is then but a barren tree. Then, so much as capacity and capability allow, ye needs must deck the tree of being with fruits such as knowledge, wisdom, spiritual perception and eloquent speech.[21]

17. Every word that proceedeth out of the mouth of God is endowed with such potency as can instil new life into every human frame, if ye be of them that comprehend this truth. All the wondrous works ye behold in this world have been manifested through the operation of His supreme and most exalted Will, His wondrous and inflexible Purpose. Through the mere revelation of the word 'Fashioner', issuing forth from His lips and proclaiming His attribute to mankind, such power is released as can generate, through successive ages, all the manifold arts which the hands of man can produce. This, verily, is a certain truth. No sooner is this resplendent word uttered, than its animating energies, stirring within all created things, give birth to the means and instruments whereby such arts can be produced and perfected. All the wondrous achievements ye now witness are the direct consequences of the Revelation of this Name.[22]

18. We prescribe unto all men that which will lead to the exaltation of the Word of God amongst His servants, and likewise, to the advancement of the world of being and the uplift of souls.

To this end, the greatest means is education of the child. To this must each and all hold fast. We have verily laid this charge upon you in manifold Tablets as well as in My Most Holy Book. Well is it with him who deferreth thereto.[23]

19. The first Ṭaráz and the first effulgence which hath dawned from the horizon of the Mother Book is that man should know his own self and recognize that which leadeth unto loftiness or lowliness, glory or abasement, wealth or poverty. Having attained the stage of fulfilment and reached his maturity, man standeth in need of wealth, and such wealth as he acquireth through crafts or professions is commendable and praiseworthy in the estimation of men of wisdom, and especially in the eyes of servants who dedicate themselves to the education of the world and to the edification of its peoples. They are, in truth, cup-bearers of the life-giving water of knowledge and guides unto the ideal way. They direct the peoples of the world to the straight path and acquaint them with that which is conducive to human upliftment and exaltation. The straight path is the one which guideth man to the dayspring of perception and to the dawning-place of true understanding and leadeth him to that which will redound to glory, honour and greatness.[24]

20. 'Unto every father hath been enjoined the instruction of his son and daughter in the art of reading and writing' (para. 48). 'Abdu'lBahá, in His Tablets, not only calls attention to the responsibility of parents to educate all their children, but He also clearly specifies that the 'training and culture of daughters is more necessary than that of sons', for girls will one day be mothers, and mothers are the first educators of the new generation. If it is not possible, therefore, for a family to educate all the children, preference is to be accorded to daughters since, through educated mothers, the benefits of knowledge can be most effectively and rapidly diffused throughout society.[25]

From the writings and talks of 'Abdu'l-Bahá

1. Were there no educator, all souls would remain savage, and were it not for the teacher, the children would be ignorant creatures.

It is for this reason that, in this new cycle, education and training are recorded in the Book of God as obligatory and not voluntary. That is, it is enjoined upon the father and mother, as a duty, to strive with all effort to train the daughter and the son, to nurse them from the breast of knowledge and to rear them in the bosom of sciences and arts. Should they neglect this matter, they shall be held responsible and worthy of reproach in the presence of the stern Lord.[26]

2. O God, O Thou Who hast cast Thy splendour over the luminous realities of men, shedding upon them the resplendent lights of knowledge and guidance, and hast chosen them out of all created things for this supernal grace, and hast caused them to encompass all things, to understand their inmost essence, and to disclose their mysteries, bringing them forth out of darkness into the visible world! 'He verily showeth His special mercy to whomsoever He will' [Qur'án 3: 67]. O Lord, help Thou Thy loved ones to acquire knowledge and the sciences and arts, and to unravel the secrets that are treasured up in the inmost reality of all created beings. Make them to hear the hidden truths that are written and embedded in the heart of all that is. Make them to be ensigns of guidance amongst all creatures, and piercing rays of the mind shedding forth their light in this, the 'first life'[Qur'án 56:62]. Make them to be leaders unto Thee, guides unto Thy path, runners urging men on to Thy Kingdom.

Thou verily art the Powerful, the Protector, the Potent, the Defender, the Mighty, the Most Generous.[27]

3. . . . every branch of learning, conjoined with the love of God, is approved and worthy of praise; but bereft of His love, learning is barren – indeed, it bringeth on madness. Every kind of knowledge, every science, is as a tree: if the fruit of it be the

love of God, then is it a blessed tree, but if not, that tree is but dried-up wood, and shall only feed the fire.[28]

4. It is clear that learning is the greatest bestowal of God; that knowledge and the acquirement thereof is a blessing from Heaven. Thus is it incumbent upon the friends of God to exert such an effort and strive with such eagerness to promote divine knowledge, culture and the sciences, that erelong those who are schoolchildren today will become the most erudite of all the fraternity of the wise. This is a service rendered unto God Himself, and it is one of His inescapable commandments.[29]

5. Now let us consider the soul. We have seen that movement is essential to existence; nothing that has life is without motion. All creation, whether of the mineral, vegetable or animal kingdom, is compelled to obey the law of motion; it must either ascend or descend. But with the human soul, there is no decline. Its only movement is towards perfection; growth and progress alone constitute the motion of the soul.

Divine perfection is infinite, therefore the progress of the soul is also infinite. From the very birth of a human being the soul progresses, the intellect grows and knowledge increases. When the body dies the soul lives on. All the differing degrees of created physical beings are limited, but the soul is limitless![30]

6. Wherefore, O loved ones of God! Make ye a mighty effort till you yourselves betoken this advancement and all these confirmations, and become focal centres of God's blessings, daysprings of the light of His unity, promoters of the gifts and graces of civilized life. Be ye in that land vanguards of the perfections of humankind; carry forward the various branches of knowledge, be active and progressive in the field of inventions and the arts. Endeavor to rectify the conduct of men, and seek to excel the whole world in moral character. While the children are yet in their infancy feed them from the breast of heavenly grace, foster them in the cradle of all excellence, rear them in the embrace of bounty. Give them the advantage of every useful

kind of knowledge. Let them share in every new and rare and wondrous craft and art. Bring them up to work and strive, and accustom them to hardship. Teach them to dedicate their lives to matters of great import, and inspire them to undertake studies that will benefit mankind.[31]

7. Among the greatest of all great services is the education of children, and promotion of the various sciences, crafts and arts. Praised be God, ye are now exerting strenuous efforts toward this end. The more ye persevere in this most important task, the more will ye witness the confirmations of God, to such a degree that ye yourselves will be astonished.[32]

8. . . . in Europe it has come to be held that religion is the enemy of science and that science is the destroyer of the foundations of religion. Whereas the religion of God is the promoter of truth, the establisher of science and learning, the supporter of knowledge, the civilizer of the human race, the discoverer of the secrets of existence, and the enlightener of the horizons of the world. How then could it oppose knowledge? God forbid! On the contrary, in the sight of God knowledge is the greatest human virtue and the noblest human perfection. To oppose knowledge is pure ignorance, and one who abhors the arts and sciences is not a human being but is even as a mindless animal. For knowledge is light, life, felicity, perfection, and beauty, and causes the soul to draw nigh to the divine threshold. It is the honour and glory of the human realm and the greatest of God's bounties. Knowledge is identical to guidance, and ignorance is the essence of error.[33]

9. All the heavenly Books, divine Prophets, sages and philosophers agree that warfare is destructive to human development, and peace constructive. They agree that war and strife strike at the foundations of humanity. Therefore, a power is needed to prevent war and to proclaim and establish the oneness of humanity.

But knowledge of the need of this power is not sufficient. Realizing that wealth is desirable is not becoming wealthy. The admission that scientific attainment is praiseworthy does not confer scientific knowledge. Acknowledgement of the excellence of honour does not make a man honourable. Knowledge of human conditions and the needed remedy for them is not the cause of their betterment. To admit that health is good does not constitute health. A skilled physician is needed to remedy existing human conditions. As a physician is required to have complete knowledge of pathology, diagnosis, therapeutics and treatment, so this World Physician must be wise, skilful and capable before health will result. His mere knowledge is not health; it must be applied and the remedy carried out.

The attainment of any object is conditioned upon knowledge, volition and action. Unless these three conditions are forthcoming, there is no execution or accomplishment.[34]

10. Although to acquire the sciences and arts is the greatest glory of mankind, this is so only on condition that man's river flow into the mighty Sea, and draw from God's ancient source His inspiration. When this cometh to pass, then every teacher is as a shoreless ocean, every pupil a prodigal fountain of knowledge. If, then, the pursuit of knowledge lead to the beauty of Him Who is the Object of all knowledge, how excellent that goal; but if not, a mere drop will perhaps shut a man off from flooding grace, for with learning cometh arrogance and pride, and it bringeth on error and indifference to God.

The sciences of this world are bridges to reality; if then they lead not to reality, naught remains but fruitless illusion. By the one true God! If learning be not a means of access to Him, the Most Manifest, it is nothing but evident loss.[35]

11. O ye beloved, and ye handmaids of the Merciful! This is the day when the Day-Star of Truth rose over the horizon of life, and its glory spread, and its brightness shone out with such power that it clove the dense and high-piled clouds and mounted the skies of the world in all its splendour. Hence do ye witness a new stirring throughout all created things.

See how, in this day, the scope of sciences and arts hath widened out, and what wondrous technical advances have been made, and to what a high degree the mind's powers have increased, and what stupendous inventions have appeared.

This age is indeed as a hundred other ages: should ye gather the yield of a hundred ages, and set that against the accumulated product of our times, the yield of this one era will prove greater than that of a hundred gone before . . . See how powerful is the influence exerted by the Day-Star of the world upon the inner essence of all created things![36]

12. All blessings are divine in origin, but none can be compared with this power of intellectual investigation and research, which is an eternal gift producing fruits of unending delight. Man is ever partaking of these fruits. All other blessings are temporary; this is an everlasting possession. Even sovereignty has its limitations and overthrow; this is a kingship and dominion which none may usurp or destroy. Briefly, it is an eternal blessing and divine bestowal, the supreme gift of God to man. Therefore, you should put forward your most earnest efforts towards the acquisition of science and arts. The greater your attainment, the higher your standard in the divine purpose. The man of science is perceiving and endowed with vision, whereas he who is ignorant and neglectful of this development is blind. The investigating mind is attentive, alive; the callous and indifferent mind is deaf and dead. A scientific man is a true index and representative of humanity, for through processes of inductive reasoning and research he is informed of all that appertains to humanity, its status, conditions and happenings. He studies the human body politic, understands social problems and weaves the web and texture of civilization. In fact, science may be likened to a mirror wherein the infinite forms and images of existing things are revealed and reflected. It is the very foundation of all individual and national development. Without this basis of investigation, development is impossible. Therefore, seek with diligent endeavour the knowledge and attainment of all that lies within the power of this wonderful bestowal.[37]

13. O true companions! All humankind are as children in a school, and the Dawning-Points of Light, the Sources of divine revelation, are the teachers, wondrous and without peer. In the school of realities they educate these sons and daughters, according to teachings from God, and foster them in the bosom of grace, so that they may develop along every line, show forth the excellent gifts and blessings of the Lord, and combine human perfections; that they may advance in all aspects of human endeavour, whether outward or inward, hidden or visible, material or spiritual, until they make of this mortal world a widespread mirror, to reflect that other world which dieth not.[38]

14. I rejoice to hear that thou takest pains with thine art, for in this wonderful new age, art is worship. The more thou strivest to perfect it, the closer wilt thou come to God. What bestowal could be greater than this, that one's art should be even as the act of worshipping the Lord? That is to say, when thy fingers grasp the paintbrush, it is as if thou wert at prayer in the Temple.[39]

15. O thou servant of the One true God! In this universal dispensation man's wondrous craftsmanship is reckoned as worship of the Resplendent Beauty. Consider what a bounty and blessing it is that craftsmanship is regarded as worship. In former times, it was believed that such skills were tantamount to ignorance, if not a misfortune, hindering man from drawing nigh unto God. Now consider how His infinite bestowals and abundant favours have changed hell-fire into blissful paradise, and a heap of dark dust into a luminous garden.

It behooveth the craftsmen of the world at each moment to offer a thousand tokens of gratitude at the Sacred Threshold, and to exert their highest endeavour and diligently pursue their professions so that their efforts may produce that which will manifest the greatest beauty and perfection before the eyes of all men.[40]

16. The harder they strive to widen the scope of their knowledge, the better and more gratifying will be the result. Let the loved

ones of God, whether young or old, whether male or female, each according to his capabilities, bestir themselves and spare no efforts to acquire the various current branches of knowledge, both spiritual and secular, and of the arts. Whensoever they gather in their meetings let their conversation be confined to learned subjects and to information on the knowledge of the day.

If they do thus, they will flood the world with the Manifest Light, and change this dusty earth into gardens of the Realm of Glory.[41]

17. It is clear that learning is the greatest bestowal of God; that knowledge and the acquirement thereof is a blessing from Heaven. Thus is it incumbent upon the friends of God to exert such an effort and strive with such eagerness to promote divine knowledge, culture and the sciences, that erelong those who are schoolchildren today will become the most erudite of all the fraternity of the wise. This is a service rendered unto God Himself, and it is one of His inescapable commandments.[42]

18. Exert every effort to acquire the various branches of knowledge and true understanding. Strain every nerve to achieve both material and spiritual accomplishments.

Encourage the children from their earliest years to master every kind of learning, and make them eager to become skilled in every art – the aim being that through the favouring grace of God, the heart of each one may become even as a mirror disclosing the secrets of the universe, penetrating the innermost reality of all things; and that each may earn world-wide fame in all branches of knowledge, science and the arts.

Certainly, certainly, neglect not the education of the children. Rear them to be possessed of spiritual qualities, and be assured of the gifts and favours of the Lord.[43]

19. O servant of Baha! Music is regarded as a praiseworthy science at the Threshold of the Almighty, so that thou mayest chant verses at large gatherings and congregations in a most

wondrous melody and raise such hymns of praise at the Mashriqu'l-Adhkar to enrapture the Concourse on High.[44]

20. Now observe that it is education that brings East and West under man's dominion, produces all these marvellous crafts, promotes these mighty arts and sciences, and gives rise to these new discoveries and undertakings. Were it not for an educator, the means of comfort, civilization, and human virtues could in no wise have been acquired. If a man is left alone in a wilderness where he sees none of his own kind, he will undoubtedly become a mere animal. It is therefore clear that an educator is needed.

But education is of three kinds: material, human and spiritual. Material education aims at the growth and development of the body, and consists in securing its sustenance and obtaining the means of its ease and comfort. This education is common to both man and animal.

Human education, however, consists in civilization and progress, that is, sound governance, social order, human welfare, commerce and industry, arts and sciences, momentous discoveries, and great undertakings, which are the central features distinguishing man from the animal.

As to divine education, it is the education of the Kingdom and consists in acquiring divine perfections. This is indeed true education, for by its virtue man becomes the focal centre of divine blessings and the embodiment of the verse 'Let Us make man in Our image, after Our likeness'. This is the ultimate goal of the world of humanity.[45]

21. All art is a gift of the Holy spirit. When this light shines through the mind of a musician, it manifests itself in beautiful harmonies. Again, shining through the mind of a poet, it is seen in fine poetry and poetic prose. When the Light of the Sun of Truth inspires the mind of a painter, he produces marvellous pictures. These gifts are fulfilling their highest purpose, when showing forth the praise of God.[46]

22. Make ye every effort to improve the Tarbíyat School and to develop order and discipline in this institution. Utilize every means to make this school a garden of the All-Merciful, from which the lights of learning will cast their beams, and wherein the children, whether Bahá'í or other, will be educated to such a degree as to become God's gifts to man, and the pride of the human race. Let them make the greatest progress in the shortest span of time, let them open wide their eyes and uncover the inner realities of all things, become proficient in every art and skill, and learn to comprehend the secrets of all things even as they are—this faculty being one of the clearly evident effects of servitude to the Holy Threshold.

It is certain that ye will make every effort to bring this about, will also draw up plans for the opening of a number of schools. These schools for academic studies must at the same time be training centres in behaviour and conduct, and they must favour character and conduct above the sciences and arts. Good behaviour and high moral character must come first, for unless the character be trained, acquiring knowledge will only prove injurious. Knowledge is praiseworthy when it is coupled with ethical conduct and virtuous character; otherwise it is a deadly poison, a frightful danger. A physician of evil character, and who betrayeth his trust, can bring on death, and become the source of numerous infirmities and diseases.[47]

23. Establish schools that are well organized and promote the fundamentals of instruction in the various branches of knowledge through teachers who are pure and sanctified, distinguished for their high standards of conduct and general excellence, and strong in faith – scholars and educators with a thorough knowledge of sciences and arts . . .

Included must be promotion of the arts, the discovery of new wonders, the expansion of trade, and the development of industry. The methods of civilization and the beautification of the country must also be encouraged . . .[48]

24. Among the safeguards of the Holy Faith is the training of

children, and this is among the weightiest of principles in all the Divine Teachings. Thus from the very beginning mothers must rear their infants in the cradle of good morals—for it is the mothers who are the first educators—so that, when the child cometh to maturity, he will prove to be endowed with all the virtues and qualities that are worthy of praise.

And further, according to the Divine commandments, every child must learn reading and writing, and acquire such branches of knowledge as are useful and necessary, as well as learning an art or skill. The utmost care must be devoted to these matters; any neglect of them, any failure to act on them, is not permissible.[49]

25. Thy letter was received. Praise be to God it imparted the good news of thy health and safety and indicated that thou art ready to enter an agricultural school. This is highly suitable. Strive as much as possible to become proficient in the science of agriculture, for in accordance with the divine teachings the acquisition of sciences and the perfection of arts are considered acts of worship. If a man engageth with all his power in the acquisition of a science or in the perfection of an art, it is as if he has been worshipping God in churches and temples. Thus as thou enterest a school of agriculture and strivest in the acquisition of that science thou art day and night engaged in acts of worship - acts that are accepted at the threshold of the Almighty. What bounty greater than this that science should be considered as an act of worship and art as service to the Kingdom of God.[50]

26. The foremost degree of comprehension in the world of nature is that of the rational soul. This power and comprehension is shared in common by all men, whether they be heedless or aware, wayward or faithful. In the creation of God, the rational soul of man encompasses and is distinguished above all other created things: It is by virtue of its nobility and distinction that it encompasses them all. Through the power of the rational soul, man can discover the realities of things, compre-

hend their properties, and penetrate the mysteries of existence. All the sciences, branches of learning, arts, inventions, institutions, undertakings, and discoveries have resulted from the comprehension of the rational soul. These were once impenetrable secrets, hidden mysteries, and unknown realities, and the rational soul gradually discovered them and brought them out of the invisible plane into the realm of the visible. This is the greatest power of comprehension in the world of nature, and the uttermost limit of its flight is to comprehend the realities, signs, and properties of contingent things.[51]

27. God's greatest gift to man is that of intellect, or understanding.

The understanding is the power by which man acquires his knowledge of the several kingdoms of creation, and of various stages of existence, as well as of much which is invisible.

Possessing this gift, he is, in himself, the sum of earlier creations – he is able to get into touch with those kingdoms; and by this gift, he can frequently, through his scientific knowledge, reach out with prophetic vision.

Intellect is, in truth, the most precious gift bestowed upon man by the Divine Bounty. Man alone, among created beings, has this wonderful power . . .

I hope that you will use *your* understanding to promote the unity and tranquillity of mankind, to give enlightenment and civilization to the people, to produce love in all around you, and to bring about the universal peace.

Study the sciences, acquire more and more knowledge. Assuredly one may learn to the end of one's life! Use your knowledge always for the benefit of others; so may war cease on the face of this beautiful earth, and a glorious edifice of peace and concord be raised. Strive that your high ideals may be realized in the Kingdom of God on earth, as they will be in Heaven.[52]

28. The subjects to be taught in children's schools are many, and for lack of time We can touch on only a few: First and most important is training in behaviour and good character; the

rectification of qualities; arousing the desire to become accomplished and acquire perfections, and to cleave unto the religion of God and stand firm in His Laws: to accord total obedience to every just government, to show forth loyalty and trustworthiness to the ruler of the time, to be well wishers of mankind, to be kind to all.

And further, as well as in the ideals of character, instruction in such arts and sciences as are of benefit, and in foreign tongues. Also, the repeating of prayers for the well-being of ruler and ruled; and the avoidance of materialistic works that are current among those who see only natural causation, and tales of love, and books that arouse the passions.

To sum up, let all the lessons be entirely devoted to the acquisition of human perfections.

Here, then, in brief are directions for the curriculum of these schools.[53]

29. The question of training the children and looking after the orphans is extremely important, but most important of all is the education of girl children, for these girls will one day be mothers, and the mother is the first teacher of the child. In whatever way she reareth the child, so will the child become, and the results of that first training will remain with the individual throughout his entire life, and it would be most difficult to alter them. And how can a mother, herself ignorant and untrained, educate her child? It is therefore clear that the education of girls is of far greater consequence than that of boys. This fact is extremely important, and the matter must be seen to with the greatest energy and dedication.

God sayeth in the Qur'án that they shall not be equals, those who have knowledge and those who have it not. Ignorance is thus utterly to be blamed, whether in male or female; indeed, in the female its harm is greater. I hope, therefore, that the friends will make strenuous efforts to educate their children, sons and daughters alike. This is verily the truth, and outside the truth there is manifestly naught save perdition.[54]

30. In this new and wondrous Cause, the advancement of all branches of knowledge is a fixed and vital principle, and the friends, one and all, are obligated to make every effort toward this end, so that the Cause of the Manifest Light may be spread abroad, and that every child, according to his need, will receive his share of the sciences and arts – until not even a single peasant's child will be found who is completely devoid of schooling.

It is essential that the fundamentals of knowledge be taught; essential that all should be able to read and write. Wherefore is this new institution most worthy of praise, and its programme to be encouraged. The hope is that other villages will take you for a model, and that in every village where there is a certain number of believers, a school will be founded where the children can study reading, writing, and basic knowledge.

This is what bringeth joy to the heart of 'Abdu'l-Bahá, cheer and peace to His soul.[55]

31. I give you my advice, and it is this: Train these children with divine exhortations. From their childhood instill in their hearts the love of God so they may manifest in their lives the fear of God and have confidence in the bestowals of God. Teach them to free themselves from human imperfections and to acquire the divine perfections latent in the heart of man. The life of man is useful if he attains the perfections of man. If he becomes the centre of the imperfections of the world of humanity, death is better than life, and nonexistence better than existence. Therefore, make ye an effort in order that these children may be rightly trained and educated and that each one of them may attain perfection in the world of humanity. Know ye the value of these children, for they are all my children.[56]

32. Man – the true man – is soul, not body; though physically man belongs to the animal kingdom, yet his soul lifts him above the rest of creation. Behold how the light of the sun illuminates the world of matter: even so doth the Divine Light shed its rays in the kingdom of the soul. The soul it is which makes the human creature a celestial entity!

By the power of the Holy Spirit, working through his soul, man is able to perceive the Divine reality of things. All great works of art and science are witnesses to this power of the Spirit.[57]

33. It is natural for the heart and spirit to take pleasure and enjoyment in all things that show forth symmetry, harmony, and perfection. For instance: a beautiful house, a well designed garden, a symmetrical line, a graceful motion, a well written book, pleasing garments – in fact, all things that have in themselves grace or beauty are pleasing to the heart and spirit – therefore, it is most certain that a true voice causes deep pleasure.[58]

34. Let your actions cry aloud to the world that you are indeed Bahá'ís, for it is actions that speak to the world and are the cause of the progress of humanity.

If we are true Bahá'ís speech is not needed. Our actions will help on the world, will spread civilization, will help the progress of science, and cause the arts to develop. Without action nothing in the material world can be accomplished, neither can words unaided advance a man in the spiritual Kingdom. It is not through lip-service only that the elect of God have attained to holiness, but by patient lives of active service they have brought light into the world.

Therefore strive that your actions day by day may be beautiful prayers. Turn towards God, and seek always to do that which is right and noble. Enrich the poor, raise the fallen, comfort the sorrowful, bring healing to the sick, reassure the fearful, rescue the oppressed, bring hope to the hopeless, shelter the destitute![59]

35. Again among His signs is the dawning sun of His knowledge, and the rising moon of His arts and skills, and His demonstrating perfection in all His ways, as testified by the learned and accomplished of many nations . . .

. . . And yet another of His signs is the wide-spreading rays of the sun of His era, the rising moon of His times in the heaven of all the ages: His day, which standeth at the summit of all days, for its rank and power, its sciences and its arts, reaching far and wide, that have dazzled the world and astonished the minds of men.

Verily is this a matter settled and established for all time.[60]

36. O ye recipients of the favors of God! In this new and wondrous Age, the unshakeable foundation is the teaching of sciences and arts. According to explicit Holy Texts, every child must be taught crafts and arts, to the degree that is needful. Wherefore, in every city and village, schools must be established and every child in that city or village is to engage in study to the necessary degree.

It followeth that whatever soul shall offer his aid to bring this about will assuredly be accepted at the heavenly Threshold, and extolled by the Company on high.

Since ye have striven hard toward this all-important end, it is my hope that ye will reap your reward from the Lord of clear tokens and signs, and that the glances of heavenly grace will turn your way.[61]

37. O ye young Bahá'í children, ye seekers after true understanding and knowledge! A human being is distinguished from an animal in a number of ways. First of all, he is made in the image of God, in the likeness of the Supernal Light, even as the Torah saith, 'Let us make man in our image, after our likeness' [Genesis 1:26]. This divine image betokeneth all the qualities of perfection whose lights, emanating from the Sun of Truth, illumine the realities of man. And among the greatest of these attributes of perfection are wisdom and knowledge. Ye must therefore put forth a mighty effort, striving by night and day and resting not for a moment, to acquire an abundant share of all the sciences and arts, that the Divine Image, which shineth out from the Sun of Truth, may illumine the mirror of the hearts of men.

It is the longing desire of 'Abdu'lBahá to see each one of you accounted as the foremost professor in the academies, and in the school of inner significances, each one becoming a leader in wisdom.[62]

38. Thou hast written about the girls' school. What was previously written still holdeth true. There can be no improvement unless the girls are brought up in schools and centres of learning, unless they are taught the sciences and other branches of knowledge, and unless they acquire the manifold arts, as necessary, and are divinely trained. For the day will come when these girls will become mothers. Mothers are the first educators of children, who establish virtues in the child's inner nature. They encourage the child to acquire perfections and goodly manners, warn him against unbecoming qualities, and encourage him to show forth resolve, firmness, and endurance under hardship, and to advance on the high road to progress. Due regard for the education of girls is, therefore, necessary. This is a very important subject, and it should be administered and organized under the aegis of the Spiritual Assembly . . .[63]

39. All the existing arts and sciences were once hidden secrets of nature. By his command and control of nature man took them out of the plane of the invisible and revealed them in the plane of visibility, whereas according to the exigencies of nature these secrets should have remained latent and concealed.[64]

40. Were there no educator, all souls would remain savage, and were it not for the teacher, the children would be ignorant creatures.

It is for this reason that, in this new cycle, education and training are recorded in the Book of God as obligatory and not voluntary. That is, it is enjoined upon the father and mother, as a duty, to strive with all effort to train the daughter and the son, to nurse them from the breast of knowledge and to rear them in the bosom of sciences and arts. Should they neglect this matter, they shall be held responsible and worthy of reproach in the presence of the stern Lord.[65]

41. Science is the first emanation from God toward man. All created beings embody the potentiality of material perfection, but the power of intellectual investigation and scientific acqui-

sition is a higher virtue specialized to man alone. Other beings and organisms are deprived of this potentiality and attainment. God has created or deposited this love of reality in man. The development and progress of a nation is according to the measure and degree of that nation's scientific attainments. Through this means its greatness is continually increased, and day by day the welfare and prosperity of its people are assured.[66]

42. Ere long the days shall come when the men addressing the women, shall say 'Blessed are ye! Blessed are ye! Verily ye are worthy of every gift. Verily ye deserve to adorn your heads with the crown of everlasting glory, because in sciences and arts, in virtues and perfections ye shall become equal to man, and as regards tenderness of heart and the abundance of mercy and sympathy ye are superior.'[67]

43. But the indispensable basis of all is that he should develop spiritual characteristics and the praiseworthy virtues of humankind. This is the primary consideration. If a person be unlettered, and yet clothed with divine excellence, and alive in the breaths of the Spirit, that individual will contribute to the welfare of society, and his inability to read and write will do him no harm. And if a person be versed in the arts and every branch of knowledge, and not live a religious life, and not take on the characteristics of God, and not be directed by a pure intent, and be engrossed in the life of the flesh – then he is harm personified, and nothing will come of all his learning and intellectual accomplishments but scandal and torment.

If, however, an individual hath spiritual characteristics, and virtues that shine out, and his purpose in life be spiritual and his inclinations be directed toward God, and he also study other branches of knowledge—then we have light upon light: his outer being luminous, his private character radiant, his heart sound, his thought elevated, his understanding swift, his rank noble.

Blessed is he who attaineth this exalted station.[68]

44. Training in morals and good conduct is far more important than book learning. A child that is cleanly, agreeable, of good character, well-behaved – even though he be ignorant – is preferable to a child that is rude, unwashed, ill-natured, and yet becoming deeply versed in all the sciences and arts. The reason for this is that the child who conducts himself well, even though he be ignorant, is of benefit to others, while an ill-natured, ill-behaved child is corrupted and harmful to others, even though he be learned. If, however, the child be trained to be both learned and good, the result is light upon light.

Children are even as a branch that is fresh and green; they will grow up in whatever way ye train them. Take the utmost care to give them high ideals and goals, so that once they come of age, they will cast their beams like brilliant candles on the world, and will not be defiled by lusts and passions in the way of animals, heedless and unaware, but instead will set their hearts on achieving everlasting honour and acquiring all the excellences of humankind.[69]

45. O ye handmaids of the Merciful! The school for girls taketh precedence over the school for boys, for it is incumbent upon the girls of this glorious era to be fully versed in the various branches of knowledge, in sciences and the arts and all the wonders of this pre-eminent time, that they may then educate their children and train them from their earliest days in the ways of perfection.

If, as she ought, the mother possesseth the learning and accomplishments of humankind, her children, like unto angels, will be fostered in all excellence, in right conduct and beauty. Therefore the School for Girls that hath been established in that place must be made the object of the deep concern and high endeavours of the friends.[70]

46. Knowledge is not enough; we hope by the Love of God we shall put it into practice. A spiritual universal Force is needed for this. Meetings are good for engendering spiritual force. To know that it is possible to reach a state of perfection, is good; to

march forward on the path is better. We know that to help the poor and to be merciful is good and pleases God, but knowledge alone does not feed the starving man, nor can the poor be warmed by knowledge or words in the bitter winter; we must give the practical help of Loving-kindness.[71]

From the writings of Shoghi Effendi

1. What Bahá'u'lláh meant primarily with 'sciences that begin and end in words' are those theological treatises and commentaries that encumber the human mind rather than help it to attain the truth. The students would devote their life to their study but still attain nowhere. Bahá'u'lláh surely never meant to include story-writing under such a category; and shorthand and typewriting are both most useful talents, very necessary in our present social and economic life.[72]

2. Praise be to God that the spirit of the Holy Writings and Tablets which have been revealed in this wondrous Dispensation concerning matters of major or minor importance, whether essential or otherwise, related to the sciences and the arts, to natural philosophy, literature, politics or economics, have so permeated the world that since the inception of the world in the course of past Dispensations and bygone ages nothing like it has ever been seen or heard. Indeed, if an avowed follower of Bahá'u'lláh were to immerse himself in, and fathom the depths of, the ocean of these heavenly teachings, and with utmost care and attention deduce from each of them the subtle mysteries and consummate wisdom that lie enshrined therein, such a person's life, materially, intellectually and spiritually, will be safe from toil and trouble, and unaffected by setbacks and perils, or any sadness or despondency.[73]

3. Every child, without exception, must from his earliest years make a thorough study of the art of reading and writing, and according to his own tastes and inclinations and the degree of his capacity and powers, devote extreme diligence to the acqui-

sition of learning beneficial arts and skills, various languages, speech, and contemporary technology.[74]

From messages and letters from the Universal House of Justice

1. The beloved Guardian made it clear that the flowering of the arts which is the result of a divine revelation comes only after a number of centuries. The Bahá'í Faith offers the world the complete rebuilding of human society – a rebuilding of such far-reaching effect that it has been looked forward to in all the revelations of the past and has been called the establishment of the Kingdom of God on earth. The new architecture to which this revelation will give birth will blossom many generations hence. We are now merely at the beginning of this great process.

The present time is a period of turmoil and change. Architecture, like all arts and sciences, is undergoing very rapid development; one has only to consider the changes that have taken place in the course of the last few decades to have some idea of what is likely to happen during the years immediately ahead. Some modern buildings have, no doubt, qualities of greatness and will endure, but very much of what is being constructed now may be outgrown and may appear ugly but a few generations hence. Modern architecture, in other words, may be considered a new development in its primitive stage.[75]

2. The same destructive forces are also deranging the political, economic, scientific, literary, and moral equilibrium of the world and are destroying the fairest fruits of the present civilization. . . . Even music, art, and literature, which are to represent and inspire the noblest sentiments and highest aspirations and should be a source of comfort and tranquillity for troubled souls, have strayed from the straight path and are now the mirrors of the soiled hearts of this confused, unprincipled, and disordered age.[76]

3. Rejecting the low sights of mediocrity let them scale the ascending heights of excellence in all they aspire to do. May

they resolve to elevate the very atmosphere in which they move, whether it be in the school rooms or halls of higher learning, in their work, their recreation, their Bahá'í activity or social service.

Indeed, let them welcome with confidence the challenges awaiting them. Imbued with this excellence and a corresponding humility, with tenacity and a loving servitude, today's youth must move towards the front ranks of the professions, trades, arts and crafts which are necessary to the further progress of humankind – this to ensure that the spirit of the Cause will cast its illumination on all these important areas of human endeavour. Moreover, while aiming at mastering the unifying concepts and swiftly advancing technologies of this era of communications, they can, indeed they must, also guarantee the transmittal to the future of those skills which will preserve the marvellous, indispensable achievements of the past. The transformation which is to occur in the functioning of society will certainly depend to a great extent on the effectiveness of the preparations the youth make for the world they will inherit.[77]

4. In much of the region, insufficient attention has been given to the education of children. Far more extensive programmes should be initiated in those countries where the need exists, to ensure that Bahá'í children are nurtured, encouraged to acquire trained minds, illumined with a sound knowledge of the Divine Teachings, well-equipped to participate in the work of the Cause at all levels and to contribute to the arts, crafts and sciences necessary for the advancement of civilization. Such programmes, when open to all children, Bahá'í or not, offer a potent means of extending the beneficial influences of Bahá'u'lláh's Message to the wider society.[78]

5. In all their efforts to achieve the aim of the Four Year Plan, the friends are also asked to give greater attention to the use of the arts, not only for proclamation, but also for the work in expansion and consolidation. The graphic and performing arts and literature have played, and can play, a major role in extend-

ing the influence of the Cause. At the level of folk art, this possibility can be pursued in every part of the world, whether it be in villages, towns or cities. Shoghi Effendi held high hopes for the arts as a means for attracting attention to the Teachings. A letter written on his behalf to an individual thus conveys the Guardian's view: "The day will come when the Cause will spread like wildfire when its spirit and teachings will be presented on the stage or in art and literature as a whole. Art can better awaken such noble sentiments than cold rationalizing, especially among the mass of the people.[79]

6. . . . there are certain fundamental concepts that all should bear in mind. One is the centrality of knowledge to social existence. The perpetuation of ignorance is a most grievous form of oppression; it reinforces the many walls of prejudice that stand as barriers to the realization of the oneness of humankind, at once the goal and operating principle of Bahá'u'lláh's Revelation. Access to knowledge is the right of every human being, and participation in its generation, application and diffusion a responsibility that all must shoulder in the great enterprise of building a prosperous world civilization--each individual according to his or her talents and abilities. Justice demands universal participation.[80]

7. Apart from the spiritual requisites of a sanctified Bahá'í life, there are habits of thought that affect the unfoldment of the global Plan, and their development has to be encouraged at the level of culture. There are tendencies, as well, that need to be gradually overcome. Many of these tendencies are reinforced by approaches prevalent in society at large, which, not altogether unreasonably, enter into Bahá'í activity. The magnitude of the challenge facing the friends in this respect is not lost on us. They are called upon to become increasingly involved in the life of society, benefiting from its educational programmes, excelling in its trades and professions, learning to employ well its tools, and applying themselves to the advancement of its arts and sciences. At the same time, they are never to lose sight

of the aim of the Faith to effect a transformation of society, remoulding its institutions and processes, on a scale never before witnessed.[81]

8. Acceptance of the teachings of Bahá'u'lláh carries with it the commitment to strive for individual spiritual maturity and to participate in collective efforts to build a thriving society and contribute to the common weal. Science and religion are the two inseparable, reciprocal systems of knowledge impelling the advancement of civilization. In the words of 'Abdu'l-Bahá, 'The progress of the world of humanity dependeth upon knowledge, and its decline is due to ignorance. When the human race gaineth in knowledge it becometh heavenly, and when it acquireth learning it taketh on lordly attributes.' To seek to acquire knowledge and learning and to study useful sciences and crafts are among the fundamental beliefs of the followers of Bahá'u'lláh. Therefore, the long-term solution you have chosen as a means of counteracting the difficulties imposed upon you in the path of higher education is to engage in constructive collaboration with other proponents of peace and reconciliation to build a progressive and orderly society committed to the promotion of knowledge and social justice.[82]

9. One of the critical aspects of a conceptual framework that will require careful attention in the years ahead is the generation and application of knowledge . . . At the heart of most disciplines of human knowledge is a degree of consensus about methodology – an understanding of methods and how to use them appropriately to systematically investigate reality to achieve reliable results and sound conclusions. Bahá'ís who are involved in various disciplines – economics, education, history, social science, philosophy, and many others – are obviously conversant and fully engaged with the methods employed in their fields. It is they who have the responsibility to earnestly strive to reflect on the implications that the truths found in the Revelation may hold for their work. The principle of the harmony of science and religion, faithfully upheld, will ensure

that religious belief does not succumb to superstition and that scientific findings are not appropriated by materialism.[83]

10. Increasingly, participation in institute courses is preparing the friends of God for an ever-deeper engagement in the life of the wider community; it is endowing them with the knowledge, insights, and skills that enable them to contribute not only to the process of developing their own community, but to the progress of society.[84]

11. When we first introduced the concept of the training institute, it was in the context of the need to raise up human resources to take on the tasks of expansion and consolidation. At this juncture, when a new series of Plans has just begun, we invite you to take a more expansive view. Increasingly, participation in institute courses is preparing the friends of God for and ever-deeper engagement in the life of the wider community; it is endowing them with the knowledge, insights, and skills that enable them to contribute not only to the process of developing their own community, but to the progress of society.[85]

12. And so the company of the faithful enter the second year of the Plan with a fresh perspective and a profound insight into the significance of what they seek to achieve. How different actions look when viewed in light of the society-building power they release! This expansive prospect allows a sustained activity to be seen as much more than an isolated act of service or just a data point. In place after place, the initiatives being pursued reveal a population learning how to take increasing responsibility for navigating the path of its own development. The resulting spiritual and social transformation manifests itself in the life of a people in a variety of ways. In the previous series of Plans, it could be seen most clearly in the promotion of spiritual education and collective worship. In this new series of Plans, increasing attention needs to be given to other processes that seek to enhance the life of a community – for example, by improving public health, protecting the environment, or

drawing more effectively on the power of the arts. What is required for all these complementary aspects of a community's well-being to advance is, of course, the capacity to engage in systematic learning in all these areas – a capacity that draws on insights arising from the Teachings and the accumulated store of human knowledge generated through scientific enquiry. As this capacity grows, much will be accomplished over the coming decades.[86]

Bibliography

'Abdu'l-Bahá. *'Abdu'l-Bahá in London* (1912, 1921). London: Bahá'í Publishing Trust, 1982.

— *Paris Talks: Addresses given by 'Abdu'l-Bahá in 1911* (1912). London: Bahá'í Publishing Trust, 12th ed. 1995.

— *The Promulgation of Universal Peace: Talks Delivered by 'Abdu'l-Baha During His Visit to the United States and Canada in 1912* (1922, 1925). Comp. H. MacNutt. Wilmette, IL: Bahá'í Publishing Trust, 2nd ed. 1982.

— *Selections from the Writings of 'Abdu'l-Bahá.* Comp. Research Department of the Universal House of Justice. Haifa: Bahá'í World Centre, 1978.

— *Some Answered Questions* (1908). Comp. and trans. Laura Clifford Barney. Haifa: Bahá'í World Centre, rev. ed. 2014.

Anderson, Chris. *TED Talks: The Official TED Guide to Public Speaking.* Hodder and Stoughton, 2018.

The Báb. *Selections from the Writings of the Báb.* Comp. Research Department of the Universal House of Justice. Haifa: Bahá'í World Centre, 1976.

Bahá'í Education. Comp. Research Department of the Universal House of Justice. Haifa: Bahá'í World Centre, 1976, rev. ed. 1990.

Bahá'í Reference Library. Authoritative online source of Bahá'í writings https://www.bahai.org/library/authoritative-texts.

Bahá'u'lláh. *The Call of the Divine Beloved: Selected Mystical Works of Bahá'u'lláh.* Haifa: Bahá'í World Centre, 2018.

— *Epistle to the Son of the Wolf.* Trans. Shoghi Effendi. Wilmette, IL: Bahá'í Publishing Trust, rev. ed. 1976.

— *The Hidden Words of Bahá'u'lláh.* Trans. Shoghi Effendi. Wilmette, IL: Bahá'í Publishing Trust, 1970; New Delhi: Bahá'í Publishing Trust, 1987.

— *The Kitáb-i-Aqdas: The Most Holy Book*. Haifa: Bahá'í World Centre, 1992.

— *Kitáb-i-Íqán: The Book of Certitude*. Trans. Shoghi Effendi. Wilmette, IL: Bahá'í Publishing Trust, 2nd ed. 1950, 1981.

— *The Summons of the Lord of Hosts: Tablets of Bahá'u'lláh*. Haifa: Bahá'í World Centre, 2002.

— *Tablets of Bahá'u'lláh Revealed after the Kitáb-i-Aqdas*. Comp. Research Department of the Universal House of Justice. Haifa: Bahá'í World Centre, 1978.

Bernstein, Richard J. *Beyond Objectivism and Relativism: Science, Hermeneutics, and Praxis*. Philadelphia: University of Pennsylvania Press, 1983.

Blomfield, Lady. *The Chosen Highway*. London: Bahá'í Publishing Trust, 1940. RP Oxford: George Ronald, 2007.

The Compilation of Compilations. Prepared by the Universal House of Justice 1963–1990. 2 vols. Sydney: Bahá'í Publications Australia, 1991.

Deutsch, David. *The Fabric of Reality*. London: Penguin. 1998.

Edwards, Betty. *Drawing on the Right Side of the Brain: A Course in Enhancing Creativity and Artistic Confidence*. 4th ed. London: Souvenir Press

Gardner, Howard E. *Five Minds for the Future*. Cambrdige, MA: Harvard Business Review Press, 2009.

— *Intelligence Reframed: Multiple Intelligences for the 21st Century*. New York: Basic Books, 2000.

Hyman, Peter. 'Anatomy of Learning', in *RSA Journal*, vol. 163, no. 3 (5571) (2017), pp. 26–3.

'The Importance of the Arts in Promoting the Faith'. Comp. Research Department of the Universal House of Justice. Haifa: Bahá'í World Centre, 1998.

Lucas, Mary L. *A Brief Account of My Visit to Acca,* Chicago: Bahai Publishing Society, 1905. RP Forgotten Books, 2018.

Momen, Moojan. 'Perfection and Refinement: Toward an Aesthetic of the Báb", first presented at the Irfán Colloquia Session 97, Centre for Bahá'í Studies, Acuto, Italy, 3-6 July 2010; in *Lights of Irfán*, vol. 12 (Irfán Colloquia, 2011), pp. 221–43. Slightly updated in 2014, available at: http://irfancolloquia.org/97/momen_refinement.

National Advisory Committee on Creative and Cultural Education (NACCCE). *All Our Futures: Creativity, Culture and Education.* London: Department for Education and Employment (DFEE), 1999.

Robinson, Ken. 'Do Schools Kill Creativity?', TED talk, 2006. Video.

— *Imagine If: Creating a Future for Us All.* London: Penguin, 2022.

— *Out of Our Minds: The Power of Being Creative.* London: Wiley, 2017.

The Ruhi Institute. *Book 7: Walking Together on a Path of Service.* Riviera Beach, FL: Palabra Publications

Saiedi, Nader. *Gate of the Heart.* Waterloo, Ont.: Wilfred Laurier University Press, 2008.

Shoghi Effendi. *The Advent of Divine Justice* (1939). Wilmette, IL: Bahá'í Publishing Trust, 1984.

— *God Passes By* (1944). Wilmette, IL: Bahá'í Publishing Trust, rev. ed. 1974.

'Social Action'. A compilation prepared by the Research Department of the Universal House of Justice. Haifa, 2020. Available at Bahá'í Reference Library.

Sonne der Wahrheit. German Bahá'í periodical published in the early 1900s.

Tuman, Ludwig. 'A New Vision for the Arts in Spiritualizing Society', paper given at the 2000 Conference on Social and Economic Development, Orlando, Florida.

The Universal House of Justice. Messages to the Bahá'ís of the World, Riḍván, 2000, 2010, 2021 and 2023. Available online at Bahá'í Reference Library.

Warwick Commission on the Future of Cultural Value, *Enriching Britain: Culture, Creativity and Growth.* The University of Warwick, United Kingdom, 2015.

Notes and References

Introduction

1 The Universal House of Justice, Message to the Bahá'ís of the World, Riḍván 2010. Available online at Bahá'í Reference Library.
2 ibid.

1 Art and Artists

1 Tuman, 'A New Vision for the Arts in Spiritualizing Society'.
2 Bahá'ú'lláh, from a Tablet translated from the Persian, in 'Extracts from the Writings concerning Arts and Crafts', in *The Compilation of Compilations*, vol. 1, p. 1, no. 2. Shoghi Effendi, the Guardian of the Bahá'í Faith, clarifies the final line regarding the sciences brought forth by words and coming to an end with words: He says that it means: 'fruitless excursions into metaphysical hair splittings' or 'those theological treatises and commentaries that encumber the human mind rather than help it to attain the truth' (see Bahá'u'lláh, *The Kitab-i-Aqdas*, note 110, p. 215).
3 The Báb, Persian Bayán, Vahid 4, in *Selections from the Writings of the Báb*, pp. 88–9.
4 The Báb, Persian Bayán, Vahid 4, Chapter 11, translated in Saiedi, *Gate of the Heart*, p. 255.
5 The Báb, Persian Bayán, Vahid 6, Chapter 3, p. 192, provisional translation by Moojan Momen, in Momen, 'Perfection and Refinement: Toward an Aesthetic of the Báb'.
6 The Báb, Persian Bayan, Vahid 3, Chapter 17, p. 103, provisional translation by Moojan Momen, ibid.
7 The Báb, Kitab al-Asma, INBA 29:621-25, available at: http://www.afnanlibrary.org/docs/persian-arabic-mss/inba/inba-vol-029/. Provisional translation by Moojan Momen, in Momen, 'Perfection and Refinement. . .'
8 The Universal House of Justice, Message to the Bahá'ís of the World, Riḍván 2010. Available online at Bahá'í Reference Library.

2 Science and Art

1 Hooper Dunbar, 'Recognizing Bahá'u'lláh on the Bi-Centenary of His Birth', presentation to the Association of Bahá'í Studies conference, 2017, video, author's transcription.
2 'Abdu'l-Bahá, *The Promulgation of Universal Peace*, p. 157.
3 Anderson, *TED Talks: The Official TED Guide to Public Speaking*, pp. 231–2.
4 ibid. p. 232.
5 Bahá'u'lláh, *Epistle to the Son of the Wolf*, pp. 26–7, quoting Bahá'u'lláh, 'Tajallíyát', in *Tablets of Bahá'u'lláh Revealed after the Kitab-i-Aqdas*, pp. 51–2.
6 Bahá'u'lláh, 'Ṭarázát (Ornaments)', *Tablets of Bahá'u'lláh Revealed after the Kitab-i-Aqdas*, p. 39.
7 Bahá'u'lláh, 'Lawḥ-i-Dunyá (Tablet of the World), ibid. p. 96.
8 'Abdu'l-Bahá, *Selections from the Writings of 'Abdu'l-Bahá*, no. 126, p. 144.
9 ibid. no. 109, pp. 134–5.
10 ibid. no. 73, p. 111.
11 The Universal House of Justice, Message to the Bahá'ís of the World, Riḍván 2010.

3 Science and Art of Human and Spiritual Capacities

1 Robinson, *Out of Our Minds*, p. 53.
2 Gardner, *Intelligence Reframed: Multiple Intelligences for the 21st Century*.
3 Robinson, 'Do Schools Kill Creativity?'
4 National Advisory Committee on Creative and Cultural Education, *All Our Futures: Creativity, Culture and Education, Defining Creativity*, p. 27.
5 ibid. p. 28.
6 ibid. p. 31.
7 Warwick Commission on the Future of Cultural Value, *Enriching Britain: Culture, Creativity and Growth*, section 4.1.2, p. 45.
8 Robinson, *Out of Our Minds*, pp. 136–7.
9 ibid. p. 131.
10 ibid. p. 138.
11 ibid. p. 1.
12 'Abdu'l-Bahá, *Paris Talks*, no. 29, p. 89
13 'Abdu'l-Bahá, *Some Answered Questions*, no. 58, pp. 250–51.
14 'Abdu'l-Bahá, *Paris Talks*, no. 28, pp. 83–4
15 Bahá'í Reference Library, Compilation for the 2018 Counsellors

Conference, no. 4: 'From a Tablet of 'Abdu'l-Bahá. translated from the Persian'.

16 'Abdu'l-Bahá, *Some Answered Questions*, no. 55, pp. 241–2.
17 'Abdu'l-Bahá, *Paris Talks*, no. 29, p. 87.
18 ibid. p. 88.
19 Letter from Dr Josephina Fallscheer to Alice Scwarz-Solivo, in *Sonne der Wahrheit* (March 1910), trans. Richard Groseer. https://bahai-library.com/fallscheer_schwarz-solivo_letter.
20 Bahá'u'lláh, 'The Valley of Wonderment' in 'The Seven Valleys', paras. 69-71, in *The Call of the Divine Beloved*, pp. 43–4.

4 Science and Art of Education

1 See Gardner, *Five Minds for the Future.*
2 Royal Society of Arts, 'Anatomy of Learning', p. 28.
3 Robinson, *Out of Our Minds.*
4 Robinson, *Imagine If*, pp. 61–2.
5 Bahá'u'lláh, 'Lawḥ-i-Maqsúd' (Tablet of Maqsúd), in *Tablets of Bahá'u'lláh Revealed after the Kitáb-i-Aqdas*, p. 162.
6 Bahá'u'lláh, *Gleanings from the Writings of Bahá'u'lláh*, CXXXII, p. 287.
7 'Abdu'l-Bahá, quoted in the compilation 'Social Action', no. 188. Available at Bahá'í Reference Library.
8 'Abdu'l-Bahá, ibid. no. 55.
9 'Abdu'l-Bahá, ibid. no. 185.
10 The Báb, Persian Bayán, Vahid 4, Chapter 11, translated in Saiedi, *Gate of the Heart*, p. 255.
11 'Abdu'l-Bahá, quoted in the compilation 'Bahá'í Education' in *The Compilation of Compilations*, vol. I, p. 251, no. 578.
12 'Abdu'l-Bahá, quoted in the compilation 'Social Action', no. 188. Available at Bahá'í Reference Library.

5 Science and Art of Bahá'í Learning Spaces

1 'The Training Institute', at https://www.bahai.org/action/response call-bahaullah/training-institute.
2 https://www.ruhi.org/en/statement-of-purpose-and-methods/.
3 The Universal House of Justice, Message to the Bahá'ís of the World, Riḍván 2010.
4 The Universal House of Justice, Message to the Bahá'ís of the World, Riḍván 2021.
5 The Universal House of Justice, Message to the Bahá'ís of the World, Riḍván 2023.

6 The Báb, Persian Bayan, Vahid 3, Chapter 17, p. 103, provisional translation by Moojan Momen, in Momen, 'Perfection and Refinement: Toward an Aesthetic of the Báb'.
7 The Ruhi Institute, Book 7, p.130.
8 ibid.
9 The Ruhi Institute, Book 7, p. 50.
10 Letter written on behalf of Shoghi Effendi to the Louhelen School, 29 July 1939, in the compilation 'Centres of Bahá'í Learning' in *The Compilation of Compilations*, vol. 1, p. 39, no. 103.
11 Letter written on behalf of Shoghi Effendi to the Green Acre Summer School. 21 October 1925, ibid. p. 25, no. 67.
12 Letter written on behalf of Shoghi Effendi to the Central States Summer School, 15 August 1938, ibid. p. 28, no. 73.
13 Letter written on behalf of Shoghi Effendi to the Bahá'ís of Esslingen, Germany, 1 October 1933, ibid. p. 41, no. 108.
14 Adapted from Shoghi Effendi, *God Passes By*, pp. 340–41.
15 The Universal House of Justice, Message to the Bahá'ís of the World, Riḍván 2023.

6 Science and Art of Life

1 Bahá'u'lláh, *The Kitáb-i-Aqdas*, para. 182, p. 85.
2 Bahá'ú'lláh, from a Tablet translated from the Persian, in the compilation 'Extracts from the Writings concerning Arts and Crafts', in *The Compilation of Compilations*, vol. 1, p. 3, no. 10.
3 Bahá'u'lláh, *Hidden Words*, Persian no. 82.
4 Bahá'u'lláh, 'Lawḥ-i-Maqsúd' (Tablet of Maqsúd), in *Tablets of Bahá'u'lláh Revealed after the Kitáb-i-Aqdas*, p. 162.
5 'Abdu'l-Bahá, quoted in Shoghi Effendi, *The Advent of Divine Justice*, p. 26.
6 Bahá'u'lláh, 'The Seven Valleys', para. 43, in *The Call of the Divine Beloved*, p. 31.
7 Bahá'u'lláh, quoted in Shoghi Effendi, *The Advent of Divine Justice*, p. 82.
8 'Abdu'l-Bahá, from a Tablet translated from the Persian, in the compilation 'The Importance of the Arts in Promoting the Faith', no. 12.
9 The Báb, Persian Bayán, Vahid 6, Chapter 3, p. 192, provisional translation by Moojan Momen, in Momen, 'Perfection and Refinement: Toward an Aesthetic of the Báb'.
10 The Báb, Kitab al-Asma, INBA 29:621-25, available at: http://www.afnanlibrary.org/docs/persian-arabic-mss/inba/inba-vol-029/.

Provisional translation by Moojan Momen, in Momen, 'Perfection and Refinement. . .'

11 Bahá'u'lláh, Kalimát-i-Firdawsíyyih (Words of Paradise), in *Tablets of Bahá'u'lláh Revealed after the Kitáb-i-Aqdas*, p. 72.

12 Bahá'u'lláh, 'The Seven Valleys', para. 70, in *The Call of the Divine Beloved*, p. 44.

13 Bahá'u'lláh, in many Bahá'í prayer books.

14 Bahá'u'lláh, from a Tablet translated from the Persian, in the compilation 'Trustworthiness, in *The Compilation of Compilations*, vol. 2, p. 332, no. 2032.

15 Bahá'u'lláh, 'Lawḥ-i-Maqsúd' (Tablet of Maqsúd), in *Tablets of Bahá'u'lláh Revealed after the Kitáb-i-Aqdas*, p. 162.

16 Shakespeare, *Hamlet*, Act 2 Sc 4.

17 Bahá'u'lláh, *Kitáb-i-Íqán*, para. 270, p. 240.

18 The Universal House of Justice, Message to the Bahá'ís of the World, Riḍván 157, 2000. Available at Bahá'í Reference Library: 'Selected Messages of the Universal House of Justice'.

19 'Abdu'l-Bahá, *Selections from the Writings of 'Abdu'l-Bahá*, no. 100, p. 127.

20 The Universal House of Justice, Message of 30 December 2021 to the Conference of the Continental Boards of Counsellors. Available at Bahá'í Reference Library: 'Selected Messages of the Universal House of Justice'.

21 The Universal House of Justice, Message to the Bahá'ís of the World, Riḍván 157, 2000, ibid.

22 'Abdu'l-Bahá, *The Promulgation of Universal Peace*, pp. 144–5.

23 'Abdu'l-Bahá, *Selections from the Writings of 'Abdu'l-Bahá*, no. 221, p. 279.

24 'Abdu'l-Bahá, *The Promulgation of Universal Peace*, p. 157.

Appendix: Arts, Science and Education: A Compilation of Bahá'í Writings

1 The Báb, Persian Bayán, Vahid 4, in *Selections from the Writings of the Báb*, pp. 88–9.

2 The Báb, Persian Bayán, Vahid 4, Chapter 11, translated in Saiedi, *Gate of the Heart*, p. 255.

3 The Báb, Persian Bayán, Vahid 6, Chapter 3, p. 192, provisional translation by Moojan Momen, in Momen, 'Perfection and Refinement: Toward an Aesthetic of the Báb'.

4 The Báb, Persian Bayán, Vahid 3, Chapter 17, p. 103, provisional translation by Moojan Momen, ibid.

5 The Báb, Kitab al-Asma, INBA 29:621-25, available at: http://www.afnanlibrary.org/docs/persian-arabic-mss/inba/inba-vol-029/. Provisional translation by Moojan Momen, in Momen, 'Perfection and Refinement. . .'
6 Bahá'u'lláh, *Gleanings from the Writings of Bahá'u'lláh*, CXXX11, p. 287.
7 Bahá'u'lláh, 'Lawḥ-i-Maqsúd' (Tablet of Maqsúd), in *Tablets of Bahá'u'lláh Revealed after the Kitáb-i-Aqdas*, p. 162.
8 ibid. pp. 168–9.
9 Bahá'u'lláh, 'Ṭarázát (Ornaments)', *Tablets of Bahá'u'lláh Revealed after the Kitab-i-Aqdas*, p. 39.
10 Bahá'u'lláh, *Epistle to the Son of the Wolf*, pp. 26–7, quoting Bahá'u'lláh, 'Tajallíyát', in *Tablets of Bahá'u'lláh Revealed after the Kitab-i-Aqdas*, pp. 51–2.
11 Bahá'u'lláh, from a Tablet translated from the Persian, in the compilation 'Excellence in All Things', in *The Compilation of Compilations*, vol. 1, p. 368, no. 771.
12 Bahá'u'lláh, *Gleanings from the Writings of Bahá'u'lláh*, LXXXII, p. 161.
13 Bahá'u'lláh, from a Tablet translated from the Persian, in the compilation 'The Importance of the Arts in Promoting the Faith', no. 1.
14 Bahá'u'lláh, Kalimát-i-Firdawsíyyih (Words of Paradise), in *Tablets of Bahá'u'lláh Revealed after the Kitáb-i-Aqdas*, p. 72.
15 Bahá'u'lláh, Lawḥ-i-Dunyá (Tablet of the World), ibid. p. 96.
16 Bahá'u'lláh, from a Tablet translated from the Arabic, in the compilation 'Extracts from the Writings concernings Arts and Crafts', in *The Compilation of Compilations*, vol. 1, p. 1, no. 5.
17 Baha'u'lláh, Súriy-i-Haykal, in Bahá'u'lláh, *The Summons of the Lord of Hosts*, pp. 35–6.
18 Bahá'u'lláh, *Epistle to the Son of the Wolf*, p. 19.
19 Bahá'ú'lláh, from a Tablet translated from the Persian, in the compilation 'Extracts from the Writings concerning Arts and Crafts', in *The Compilation of Compilations*, vol. 1, p. 1, no. 2. Shoghi Effendi, the Guardian of the Bahá'í Faith, clarifies the final line regarding the sciences brought forth by words and coming to an end with words – see the next quotation.
20 Bahá'u'lláh, *The Kitáb-i-Aqdas*, note 110, pp. 214–15.
21 Bahá'u'lláh, from a Tablet translated from the Persian, in the compilation 'Excellence in All Things', in *The Compilation of Compilations*, vol. 1, p. 368, no. 770.
22 Baha'u'lláh, *Gleanings from the Writings of Bahá'u'lláh*, LXX1V, pp.

141–2.
23 Bahá'u'lláh, from a Tablet translated from the Persian, in the compilation 'Bahá'í Education', in *The Compilation of Compilations*, vol. 1, p. 246, no. 557.
24 Bahá'u'lláh, Ṭarázát (Ornaments), in *Tablets of Bahá'u'lláh Revealed after the Kitáb-i-Aqdas*, pp. 35–5.
25 Bahá'u'lláh, *The Kitáb-i-Aqdas*, note 76, pp. 199–200.
26 'Abdu'l-Bahá, *Selections from the Writings of 'Abdu'l-Bahá*, no. 98, pp. 126–7.
27 'Abdu'l-Bahá, from a Tablet translated from the Arabic, in the compilation 'Bahá'í Education', in *The Compilation of Compilations*, vol. 1, pp. 251–2, no. 578.
28 'Abdu'l-Bahá, *Selections from the Writings of 'Abdu'l-Bahá*, no. 154, p. 181.
29 'Abdu'l-Bahá, from a Tablet translated from the Persian, in the compilation 'Social Action', no. 56.
30 'Abdu'l-Bahá, *Paris Talks*, no. 29, p. 87.
31 'Abdu'l-Bahá, *Selections from the Writings of 'Abdu'l-Bahá*, no. 102, p. 129.
32 'Abdu'l-Bahá, from a Tablet translated from the Persian, in the compilation 'The Importance of the Arts in Promoting the Faith', no. 13.
33 'Abdu'l-Bahá, *Some Answered Questions*, ch. 34, pp. 154–5.
34 'Abdu'l-Bahá, *The Promulgation of Universal Peace*, p. 157.
35 'Abdu'l-Bahá, *Selections from the Writings of 'Abdu'l-Bahá*, no. 72, p. 110 (revised version as found at Bahá'í Reference Library).
36 ibid. no. 73, p. 111.
37 'Abdu'l-Bahá, *The Promulgation of Universal Peace*, p. 50.
38 'Abdu'l-Bahá, *Selections from the Writings of 'Abdu'l-Bahá*, no. 102, p. 128.
39 'Abdu'l-Bahá, from a Tablet translated from the Persian, in the compilation 'The Importance of the Arts in Promoting the Faith', no. 12.
40 'Abdu'l-Bahá, *Selections from the Writings of 'Abdu'l-Bahá*, no. 126, p. 145.
41 'Abdu'l-Bahá, from a Tablet translated from the Arabic, in the compilation 'Excellence in All Things', in *The Compilation of Compilations*, vol. 1, p. 374, no. 789.
42 'Abdu'l-Bahá, from a Tablet translated from the Persian, ibid. no. 790.
43 'Abdu'l-Bahá, in the compilation 'Social Action', no. 188.

44 'Abdu'l-Bahá, from a Tablet translated from the Persian, in the compilation 'The Importance of the Arts in Promoting the Faith', no. 11.
45 'Abdu'l-Bahá, *Some Answered Questions*, ch. 3, p. 9.
46 'Abdu'l-Bahá, quoted in Blomfield, *The Chosen Highway*, p. 167.
47 'Abdu'l-Bahá, from a Tablet translated from the Persian, in the compilation 'Social Action', no. 190.
48 'Abdu'l-Bahá, ibid. no. 185.
49 'Abdu'l-Bahá, from a Tablet translated from the Persian, in the compilation 'Bahá'í Education', in *The Compilation of Compilations*, vol. 1, p. 262, no. 590.
50 'Abdu'l-Bahá, *Selections from the Writings of 'Abdu'l-Bahá*, no. 126, p. 144.
51 'Abdu'l-Bahá, *Some Answered Questions*, no. 58, pp. 250–51.
52 'Abdu'l-Bahá, *Paris Talks*, no. 11, pp. 32-4.
53 'Abdu'l-Bahá, from a Tablet translated from the Persian, in the compilation 'Social Action', no. 191.
54 'Abdu'l-Bahá, from a Tablet translated from the Arabic and Persian, ibid. no. 192.
55 'Abdu'l-Bahá, from a Tablet translated from the Persian, in the compilation 'Bahá'í Education', in *The Compilation of Compilations*, vol. 1, p. 279, no. 624.
56 'Abdu'l-Bahá, *The Promulgation of Universal Peace*, p. 53.
57 'Abdu'l-Bahá, *Paris Talks*, no. 28, pp. 82–3.
58 'Abdu'l-Bahá, quote in Lucas, *A Brief Account of My Visit to Acca*, p. 11.
59 'Abdu'l-Bahá, *Paris Talks*, no. 27, pp. 77–8.
60 'Abdu'l-Bahá, *Selections from the Writings of 'Abdu'l-Bahá*, no. 4, pp. 15, 17.
61 ibid. no. 109, pp. 134–5.
62 ibid. no. 118, pp. 140–41 (revised version as found at Bahá'í Reference Library).
63 'Abdu'l-Bahá, from a Tablet translated from the Persian, in the compilation 'Women', in *The Compilation of Compilations*, vol. 2, p. 374, no. 2132.
64 'Abdu'l-Bahá, *The Promulgation of Universal Peace*, p. 81.
65 'Abdu'l-Bahá, *Selections from the Writings of 'Abdu'l-Bahá*, no. 98, pp. 126–7.
66 'Abdu'l-Bahá, *The Promulgation of Universal Peace*, p. 49.
67 'Abdu'l-Bahá, *Paris Talks*, no. 59, p. 197.
68 'Abdu'l-Bahá, from a Tablet translated from the Persian, in the com-

pilation 'Bahá'í Education', in *The Compilation of Compilations*, vol. 1, p. 282, no. 627.

69 'Abdu'l-Bahá, *Selections from the Writings of 'Abdu'l-Bahá*, no. 110, pp. 135–6.

70 'Abdu'l-Bahá, from a Tablet translated from the Persian, in the compilation 'Bahá'í Education', in *The Compilation of Compilations*, vol. 1, p. 284, no. 631.

71 'Abdu'l-Bahá, *'Abdu'l-Bahá in London*, pp. 60–61.

72 Letter on behalf of Shoghi Effendi to an individual, 30 November 1932, in the compilation 'Extracts from the Bahá'í Writings on the Subject of Writers and Writing', in *The Compilation of Compilations*, vol. 2, p. 411, no. 2224.

73 Letter from Shoghi Effendi to the Bahá'ís of A<u>dh</u>irbayján, 13 January 1923, in the compilation 'The Importance of Deepening Our Knowledge and Understanding of the Faith', in *The Compilation of Compilations*, vol. 1, p. 204, no. 427.

74 Letter from Shoghi Effendi to the National Spiritual Assembly of Persia, 8 June 1925, in the compilation 'Bahá'í Education', ibid. p. 296, no. 656.

75 Letter from the Universal House of Justice to an individual, 18 July 1974, in the compilation 'The Importance of the Arts in Promoting the Faith', no. 47.

76 Letter from the Universal House of Justice to the Iranian Bahá'ís throughout the World, 10 February 1980, in Messages from the Universal House of Justice 1963–1986, p. 435; also in the compilation 'The Importance of the Arts in Promoting the Faith', no. 50.

77 Letter from the Universal House of Justice to the Bahá'í Youth of the World, 8 May 1985, ibid. no. 56.

78 Letter from the Universal House of Justice to the Followers of Bahá'u'lláh in Australasia, 21 April 1996, ibid. no. 70.

79 The Universal House of Justice, Message to the Bahá'ís of the World, Riḍván 1996. Available at Bahá'í Reference Library: 'Selected Messages of the Universal House of Justice'.

80 The Universal House of Justice, Message to the Bahá'ís of the World, Riḍván 2010, ibid.

81 The Universal House of Justice, Message of 28 December 2010 to the Conference of the Continental Boards of Counsellors, ibid.

82 The Universal House of Justice, Message of 17 June 2011 to the Believers in the Cradle of the Faith, ibid.

83 Letter on behalf of the Universal House of Justice to the National Spiritual Assembly of the Bahá'ís of Canada, 24 July 2013, ibid.

84 The Universal House of Justice, Message to the Bahá'ís of the World, Riḍván 2021, ibid.
85 The Universal House of Justice, Message of 30 December 2021 to the Conference of the Continental Boards of Counsellors, ibid.
86 The Universal House of Justice, Message to the Bahá'ís of the World, Riḍván 2023, ibid.

www.ingramcontent.com/pod-product-compliance
Lightning Source LLC
LaVergne TN
LVHW052340100826
845147LV00021B/1129

* 9 7 8 0 8 5 3 9 8 6 6 9 0 *